50 Ultra G Cake Recipes for Home

By: Kelly Johnson

Table of Contents

- Baklava Cake
- Revani (Semolina Cake)
- Karpatka (Polish Cream Cake)
- Kardinalschnitten (Cardinal Slices)
- Kataifi Cake
- Portokalopita (Orange Phyllo Cake)
- Kek with Mastiha
- Loukoum Cake
- Melomakarona Cake
- Vasilopita (New Year's Cake)
- Galaktoboureko Cake
- Tiramisù Greek Style
- Pasta Flora (Greek Jam Tart)
- Kamilaki Cake (Greek Yogurt Cake)
- Sokolatina (Chocolate Cake)
- Rizogalo Cake (Rice Pudding Cake)
- Spoon Sweet Cake
- Chocolatina
- Panzaroti Cake
- Amoita Cake
- Kourabiedes Cake
- Kremasti Cake
- Sour Cherry Cake
- Almond Cake (Amygdalopita)
- Baklava Cheesecake
- Lemon Phyllo Cake
- Zacharopita (Sweet Cake)
- Chocolatopita
- Kokkinopita (Red Cake)
- Phyllo-Wrapped Pumpkin Cake
- Pavlova Greek Style
- Cheese Pie Cake
- Greek Apple Cake
- Nuts and Honey Cake
- Honey Cake with Nuts
- Pistachio Cake

- Date Cake
- Greek Walnut Cake
- Mastic Cake
- Pistachio-Lemon Cake
- Rosewater Cake
- Fig Cake
- Greek Cream Cake
- Almond and Orange Cake
- Lemon Honey Cake
- Greek Yogurt and Honey Cake
- Greek Chocolate and Nut Cake
- Baklava Bundt Cake
- Olive Oil Cake
- Pomegranate Cake

Baklava Cake

Ingredients

For the Cake:

- 1 ½ cups all-purpose flour
- 1 tsp baking powder
- ½ tsp baking soda
- ¼ tsp salt
- ½ cup unsalted butter, softened
- ½ cup granulated sugar
- ½ cup packed brown sugar
- 2 large eggs
- 1 cup Greek yogurt or sour cream
- 1 tsp vanilla extract
- 1 cup chopped nuts (such as walnuts, pistachios, or almonds)

For the Syrup:

- 1 cup granulated sugar
- ½ cup water
- ¼ cup honey
- 1 tsp lemon juice
- 1 tsp ground cinnamon
- 1 tsp vanilla extract

For the Topping:

- 1 cup chopped nuts (such as walnuts, pistachios, or almonds)
- ¼ cup melted butter
- 1 tsp ground cinnamon

Instructions

1. **Preheat the Oven:**
    - Preheat your oven to 350°F (175°C). Grease and flour a 9-inch round cake pan or a 9x9-inch square pan.
2. **Prepare the Cake Batter:**
    - In a medium bowl, whisk together the flour, baking powder, baking soda, and salt.
    - In a large bowl, cream the softened butter, granulated sugar, and brown sugar until light and fluffy.
    - Beat in the eggs one at a time, followed by the Greek yogurt (or sour cream) and vanilla extract.
    - Gradually add the dry ingredients to the wet ingredients, mixing until just combined.

- Fold in the chopped nuts.
3. **Bake the Cake:**
    - Pour the batter into the prepared pan and smooth the top.
    - Bake for 25-30 minutes, or until a toothpick inserted into the center comes out clean.
    - Allow the cake to cool in the pan for 10 minutes before transferring it to a wire rack to cool completely.
4. **Prepare the Syrup:**
    - While the cake is baking, combine the sugar, water, honey, lemon juice, and cinnamon in a small saucepan.
    - Bring to a boil over medium heat, then reduce the heat and simmer for 10 minutes, or until slightly thickened.
    - Remove from heat and stir in the vanilla extract.
5. **Prepare the Topping:**
    - Mix the chopped nuts with melted butter and ground cinnamon in a small bowl.
6. **Assemble the Cake:**
    - Once the cake has cooled, drizzle the syrup evenly over the top.
    - Sprinkle the nut topping over the syrup.
7. **Serve:**
    - Allow the cake to absorb the syrup for at least 30 minutes before slicing and serving.

Enjoy your Baklava Cake! It's a wonderful blend of the sweet, nutty flavors of baklava with the soft, tender texture of cake.

Revani (Semolina Cake)

Ingredients

For the Cake:

- 1 cup semolina
- 1 cup all-purpose flour
- 1 cup granulated sugar
- 1 cup plain yogurt
- 3 large eggs
- 1 cup unsalted butter, melted
- 1 tsp baking powder
- 1 tsp vanilla extract
- Zest of 1 lemon (optional)

For the Syrup:

- 1 cup granulated sugar
- 1 cup water
- 1 tsp lemon juice
- 1 tsp vanilla extract

Instructions

1. **Preheat the Oven:**
    - Preheat your oven to 350°F (175°C). Grease and flour a 9x13-inch baking pan.
2. **Prepare the Cake Batter:**
    - In a large bowl, whisk together the semolina, flour, baking powder, and sugar.
    - In another bowl, beat the eggs, then mix in the yogurt, melted butter, vanilla extract, and lemon zest (if using).
    - Combine the wet and dry ingredients, mixing until smooth.
3. **Bake the Cake:**
    - Pour the batter into the prepared pan and spread evenly.
    - Bake for 30-35 minutes, or until a toothpick inserted into the center comes out clean and the top is golden brown.
4. **Prepare the Syrup:**
    - While the cake is baking, combine the sugar, water, and lemon juice in a saucepan.
    - Bring to a boil, then reduce the heat and simmer for 10 minutes.
    - Remove from heat and stir in the vanilla extract. Let it cool.
5. **Syrup the Cake:**
    - Once the cake is done baking, remove it from the oven.
    - Immediately pour the cooled syrup evenly over the hot cake.
6. **Cool and Serve:**

    - Allow the cake to cool completely and absorb the syrup before slicing and serving.

Enjoy the moist, sweet delight of Revani!

Karpatka (Polish Cream Cake)

Ingredients

For the Pastry:

- 1 cup water
- ½ cup unsalted butter
- 1 cup all-purpose flour
- 4 large eggs

For the Cream Filling:

- 2 cups milk
- 1 cup granulated sugar
- 3 large egg yolks
- ¼ cup cornstarch
- 1 tsp vanilla extract
- 4 tbsp unsalted butter, room temperature

Instructions

1. **Prepare the Pastry:**
    - Preheat your oven to 375°F (190°C). Line two baking sheets with parchment paper.
    - In a medium saucepan, bring the water and butter to a boil over medium heat.
    - Remove from heat and stir in the flour all at once. Return to heat and cook, stirring constantly, for about 2 minutes until the mixture forms a ball and pulls away from the sides of the pan.
    - Transfer the mixture to a large bowl and let it cool slightly.
    - Beat in the eggs, one at a time, making sure each is fully incorporated before adding the next. The dough should be smooth and glossy.
    - Divide the dough between the two prepared baking sheets, spreading it out evenly.
    - Bake for 20-25 minutes, or until the pastry is golden brown and crisp. Let the pastries cool completely on a wire rack.
2. **Prepare the Cream Filling:**
    - In a medium saucepan, heat the milk over medium heat until it is just about to boil.
    - In a separate bowl, whisk together the sugar, egg yolks, and cornstarch until smooth.
    - Slowly pour the hot milk into the egg mixture, whisking constantly to temper the eggs.
    - Return the mixture to the saucepan and cook over medium heat, whisking constantly, until it thickens and begins to bubble.

- Remove from heat and stir in the vanilla extract and butter until smooth. Let the cream cool to room temperature.
3. **Assemble the Cake:**
    - Place one of the cooled pastry sheets on a serving platter.
    - Spread the cream filling evenly over the pastry.
    - Top with the second pastry sheet, pressing down gently to adhere.
4. **Serve:**
    - Refrigerate the cake for at least 2 hours before slicing to allow the cream to set.
    - Optionally, dust with powdered sugar before serving.

Enjoy your Karpatka, a delightful Polish treat with its crispy layers and creamy filling!

Kardinalschnitten (Cardinal Slices)

Ingredients

For the Meringue Layers:

- 4 large egg whites
- 1 cup granulated sugar
- 1 tsp lemon juice
- 1 tsp vanilla extract
- 1 cup finely ground almonds (or almond flour)

For the Cream Filling:

- 1 cup milk
- 1 cup heavy cream
- 3 large egg yolks
- ½ cup granulated sugar
- 2 tbsp cornstarch
- 1 tsp vanilla extract
- 2 tbsp unsalted butter

For the Decoration:

- Powdered sugar, for dusting
- Fresh berries or fruit, optional

Instructions

1. **Prepare the Meringue Layers:**
    - Preheat your oven to 275°F (135°C). Line two baking sheets with parchment paper.
    - In a clean, dry bowl, beat the egg whites with lemon juice until soft peaks form.
    - Gradually add the granulated sugar, beating until stiff, glossy peaks form.
    - Gently fold in the ground almonds and vanilla extract.
    - Divide the meringue mixture evenly between the two baking sheets, spreading it into rectangles about 1/2 inch thick. Aim for an even surface.
    - Bake for 1 hour, or until the meringue is crisp and dry. Turn off the oven and let the meringues cool completely in the oven with the door slightly ajar.
2. **Prepare the Cream Filling:**
    - In a medium saucepan, heat the milk and heavy cream over medium heat until just about to boil.
    - In a bowl, whisk together the egg yolks, sugar, and cornstarch until smooth.
    - Gradually whisk the hot milk mixture into the egg mixture to temper the eggs.

- Return the mixture to the saucepan and cook over medium heat, whisking constantly, until it thickens and begins to bubble. It should be similar to a thick custard.
- Remove from heat and stir in the vanilla extract and butter until smooth. Let the cream cool to room temperature.

3. **Assemble the Cardinal Slices:**
   - Place one of the meringue layers on a serving platter.
   - Spread half of the cream filling evenly over the meringue.
   - Top with the second meringue layer, pressing down gently.
   - Spread the remaining cream filling over the top layer.
4. **Decoration and Serving:**
   - Dust the top with powdered sugar before serving.
   - Optionally, garnish with fresh berries or fruit.
5. **Chill:**
   - Chill the assembled Kardinalschnitten in the refrigerator for at least 2 hours before slicing. This allows the cream to set and makes it easier to cut into neat slices.

Enjoy your Kardinalschnitten—a refined and delightful dessert with a perfect balance of meringue and creamy filling!

Kataifi Cake

Ingredients

For the Cake:

- 1 pound (450g) kataifi dough (shredded phyllo dough), thawed
- 1 cup unsalted butter, melted
- 1 cup chopped nuts (such as walnuts, almonds, or pistachios)
- 1 cup granulated sugar
- 1 tsp ground cinnamon
- 1 tsp vanilla extract

For the Syrup:

- 1 cup granulated sugar
- 1 cup water
- 1/4 cup honey
- 1 tsp lemon juice
- 1 tsp vanilla extract

Instructions

1. **Prepare the Syrup:**
    - In a medium saucepan, combine the sugar, water, honey, and lemon juice.
    - Bring to a boil over medium heat, then reduce the heat and let it simmer for about 10 minutes until slightly thickened.
    - Remove from heat and stir in the vanilla extract. Allow the syrup to cool to room temperature.
2. **Prepare the Cake:**
    - Preheat your oven to 350°F (175°C). Grease a 9x13-inch baking pan or a similar-sized dish.
    - In a large bowl, combine the kataifi dough with the melted butter, making sure the dough is well coated.
    - Add the chopped nuts, granulated sugar, ground cinnamon, and vanilla extract. Mix until evenly distributed.
    - Spread half of the kataifi mixture evenly in the bottom of the prepared baking pan.
    - Bake for about 20 minutes, or until the top starts to turn golden brown.
3. **Layer the Cake:**
    - Remove the pan from the oven and spread the remaining kataifi mixture over the partially baked layer.
    - Return to the oven and bake for an additional 20-25 minutes, or until the top is golden brown and crispy.
4. **Add the Syrup:**

        - Immediately after removing the cake from the oven, pour the cooled syrup evenly over the hot cake.
        - Allow the cake to cool completely in the pan. The syrup will soak into the layers, making them sweet and moist.
 5. **Serve:**
        - Once cooled, cut into squares or diamond-shaped pieces and serve.

Kataifi Cake is wonderfully crispy and sweet, with a lovely nutty flavor. It's a great addition to any dessert table and pairs perfectly with a cup of coffee or tea. Enjoy!

Portokalopita (Orange Phyllo Cake)

Ingredients

For the Cake:

- 1 package (16 oz) phyllo dough, thawed
- 1 cup plain Greek yogurt
- 1 cup granulated sugar
- 4 large eggs
- 1 cup freshly squeezed orange juice
- 1 tbsp grated orange zest
- 1 tsp vanilla extract
- 1 tsp baking powder
- ½ cup unsalted butter, melted

For the Orange Syrup:

- 1 cup granulated sugar
- 1 cup water
- ½ cup freshly squeezed orange juice
- 1 tsp lemon juice
- 1 tsp vanilla extract

Optional Garnish:

- Powdered sugar, for dusting
- Orange slices or zest, for decoration

Instructions

1. **Prepare the Orange Syrup:**
    - In a medium saucepan, combine the sugar, water, orange juice, and lemon juice.
    - Bring to a boil over medium heat, stirring until the sugar is dissolved.
    - Reduce the heat and simmer for about 10 minutes until slightly thickened.
    - Remove from heat and stir in the vanilla extract. Allow the syrup to cool to room temperature.
2. **Prepare the Cake Batter:**
    - Preheat your oven to 350°F (175°C). Grease and flour a 9x13-inch baking pan or a similar-sized dish.
    - In a large bowl, whisk together the Greek yogurt, granulated sugar, eggs, orange juice, orange zest, and vanilla extract.
    - Stir in the baking powder.
    - Tear the phyllo dough into small pieces and add to the mixture, gently folding to combine. The dough should be well-coated with the liquid.
3. **Assemble and Bake the Cake:**

- Pour the batter into the prepared baking pan and spread it out evenly.
- Drizzle the melted butter over the top of the batter.
- Bake for 45-55 minutes, or until the cake is golden brown and a toothpick inserted into the center comes out clean.

4. **Add the Syrup:**
    - Immediately after removing the cake from the oven, pour the cooled orange syrup evenly over the hot cake.
    - Allow the cake to cool completely in the pan. The syrup will soak into the layers, making them moist and flavorful.

5. **Serve:**
    - Once cooled, cut into squares or slices.
    - Optionally, dust with powdered sugar and garnish with orange slices or zest before serving.

Enjoy the refreshing and flavorful Portokalopita! Its blend of crispy phyllo and sweet orange syrup makes it a perfect dessert for any occasion.

Kek with Mastiha

Ingredients

For the Cake:

- 1 cup all-purpose flour
- 1 ½ tsp baking powder
- ¼ tsp salt
- ½ cup unsalted butter, softened
- 1 cup granulated sugar
- 3 large eggs
- 1 cup Greek yogurt or sour cream
- 1 tsp vanilla extract
- 1 tbsp mastiha (mastic) powder, finely ground
- 1 tbsp milk (if needed, for thinning the batter)

For the Syrup (Optional):

- ½ cup granulated sugar
- ¼ cup water
- 1 tbsp mastiha (mastic) powder
- 1 tsp lemon juice

Instructions

1. **Prepare the Cake Batter:**
    - Preheat your oven to 350°F (175°C). Grease and flour a 9x9-inch baking pan or an 8-inch round pan.
    - In a medium bowl, whisk together the flour, baking powder, and salt.
    - In a large bowl, cream the softened butter and granulated sugar until light and fluffy.
    - Beat in the eggs one at a time, making sure each is fully incorporated before adding the next.
    - Mix in the Greek yogurt (or sour cream) and vanilla extract.
    - Gradually add the dry ingredients to the wet ingredients, mixing until just combined.
    - Fold in the mastiha powder. If the batter is too thick, add a tablespoon of milk to achieve a smooth consistency.
2. **Bake the Cake:**
    - Pour the batter into the prepared pan and smooth the top.
    - Bake for 30-35 minutes, or until a toothpick inserted into the center comes out clean and the cake is golden brown.
    - Allow the cake to cool in the pan for 10 minutes before transferring it to a wire rack to cool completely.

3. **Prepare the Syrup (Optional):**
    - In a small saucepan, combine the sugar, water, and mastiha powder.
    - Bring to a boil over medium heat, stirring until the sugar is dissolved.
    - Reduce the heat and simmer for about 5 minutes.
    - Remove from heat and stir in the lemon juice. Let the syrup cool slightly.
4. **Add the Syrup (Optional):**
    - If using syrup, brush or pour the cooled syrup evenly over the cooled cake. This adds extra moisture and a more intense mastiha flavor.
5. **Serve:**
    - Slice and serve the cake. It can be enjoyed as a light dessert or with a cup of coffee or tea.

The unique flavor of mastiha in this cake offers a wonderful and exotic twist, making Kek with Mastiha a memorable treat!

Loukoum Cake

Ingredients

For the Cake:

- 1 ½ cups all-purpose flour
- 1 cup granulated sugar
- 1 cup plain Greek yogurt
- 4 large eggs
- ½ cup unsalted butter, melted
- 1 tsp baking powder
- 1 tsp vanilla extract
- 1 tsp rose water or orange blossom water (optional, for an authentic flavor)
- 1 cup chopped loukoum (Turkish delight), diced into small pieces

For the Syrup:

- 1 cup granulated sugar
- ½ cup water
- 1 tbsp lemon juice
- 1 tsp rose water or orange blossom water (optional)

For the Garnish:

- Powdered sugar, for dusting
- Additional chopped loukoum, for decoration (optional)

Instructions

1. **Prepare the Cake Batter:**
    - Preheat your oven to 350°F (175°C). Grease and flour a 9x13-inch baking pan or an 8-inch round pan.
    - In a medium bowl, whisk together the flour and baking powder.
    - In a large bowl, beat the eggs and sugar until light and fluffy.
    - Mix in the Greek yogurt, melted butter, vanilla extract, and rose water or orange blossom water (if using).
    - Gradually add the dry ingredients to the wet ingredients, mixing until just combined.
    - Fold in the chopped loukoum pieces.
2. **Bake the Cake:**
    - Pour the batter into the prepared pan and smooth the top.
    - Bake for 30-35 minutes, or until a toothpick inserted into the center comes out clean and the cake is golden brown.
    - Allow the cake to cool in the pan for 10 minutes before transferring it to a wire rack to cool completely.

3. **Prepare the Syrup:**
    - In a small saucepan, combine the sugar, water, and lemon juice.
    - Bring to a boil over medium heat, stirring until the sugar is completely dissolved.
    - Reduce the heat and simmer for about 5 minutes.
    - Remove from heat and stir in the rose water or orange blossom water (if using). Let the syrup cool slightly.
4. **Add the Syrup:**
    - Once the cake has cooled, drizzle or brush the cooled syrup evenly over the cake. The syrup will soak into the cake, adding moisture and sweetness.
5. **Garnish and Serve:**
    - Dust the top with powdered sugar and optionally, decorate with additional chopped loukoum pieces.
    - Slice and serve.

Loukoum Cake offers a fragrant, sweet experience with a lovely texture and flavor that reflects the essence of traditional Turkish delight. Enjoy this unique and flavorful cake!

Melomakarona Cake

Ingredients

For the Cake:

- 2 ¼ cups all-purpose flour
- 1 tsp baking powder
- 1 tsp baking soda
- ¼ tsp salt
- 1 cup granulated sugar
- ½ cup unsalted butter, softened
- 1 cup olive oil
- 2 large eggs
- 1 cup freshly squeezed orange juice
- 1 tsp ground cinnamon
- ½ tsp ground cloves
- ¼ tsp ground nutmeg
- 1 cup finely chopped walnuts or almonds (optional)

For the Syrup:

- 1 cup granulated sugar
- 1 cup water
- ½ cup honey
- 1 tsp ground cinnamon
- 1 tsp lemon juice
- 1 tsp vanilla extract

For the Topping:

- ½ cup chopped walnuts or almonds
- ¼ cup honey (for drizzling)

Instructions

1. **Prepare the Cake Batter:**
    - Preheat your oven to 350°F (175°C). Grease and flour a 9x13-inch baking pan or two 8-inch round pans.
    - In a medium bowl, whisk together the flour, baking powder, baking soda, salt, ground cinnamon, ground cloves, and ground nutmeg.
    - In a large bowl, cream together the sugar, softened butter, and olive oil until light and fluffy.
    - Beat in the eggs one at a time.
    - Gradually mix in the orange juice.
    - Add the dry ingredients to the wet ingredients, mixing until just combined.

- Fold in the chopped walnuts or almonds if using.
2. **Bake the Cake:**
   - Pour the batter into the prepared pan(s) and spread evenly.
   - Bake for 30-35 minutes, or until a toothpick inserted into the center comes out clean and the top is golden brown.
   - Allow the cake to cool in the pan for 10 minutes before transferring it to a wire rack to cool completely.
3. **Prepare the Syrup:**
   - In a medium saucepan, combine the sugar, water, honey, ground cinnamon, and lemon juice.
   - Bring to a boil over medium heat, stirring until the sugar is dissolved.
   - Reduce the heat and simmer for about 10 minutes, until slightly thickened.
   - Remove from heat and stir in the vanilla extract. Let the syrup cool slightly.
4. **Add the Syrup:**
   - Once the cake has cooled, use a toothpick or skewer to poke holes all over the top of the cake.
   - Drizzle or brush the cooled syrup evenly over the cake, allowing it to soak in.
5. **Add the Topping:**
   - Sprinkle the top of the cake with chopped walnuts or almonds.
   - Drizzle with additional honey if desired.
6. **Serve:**
   - Slice and serve the cake. It's wonderful on its own or with a cup of coffee or tea.

Enjoy your Melomakarona Cake, a delicious and festive twist on the classic Greek holiday treat!

Vasilopita (New Year's Cake)

Ingredients

For the Cake:

- 1 ½ cups all-purpose flour
- 1 tsp baking powder
- ¼ tsp salt
- 1 cup granulated sugar
- ½ cup unsalted butter, softened
- 4 large eggs
- 1 cup milk
- 1 tsp vanilla extract
- 1 tbsp orange zest (optional)
- 1 tbsp brandy or orange liqueur (optional)
- 1 whole almond or coin wrapped in foil (for good luck)

For the Glaze:

- 1 cup powdered sugar
- 2-3 tbsp milk
- 1 tsp vanilla extract

For Decoration:

- Whole almonds
- Powdered sugar (for dusting)

Instructions

1. **Prepare the Cake Batter:**
    - Preheat your oven to 350°F (175°C). Grease and flour a 9-inch round cake pan or a similar-sized pan.
    - In a medium bowl, whisk together the flour, baking powder, and salt.
    - In a large bowl, cream the softened butter and granulated sugar until light and fluffy.
    - Beat in the eggs one at a time, ensuring each is fully incorporated.
    - Mix in the milk, vanilla extract, and orange zest (if using).
    - Gradually add the dry ingredients to the wet ingredients, mixing until just combined.
    - Stir in the brandy or orange liqueur if using.
2. **Add the Coin:**
    - Carefully place the wrapped coin or almond into the batter. Gently mix to distribute it evenly, but be careful not to overmix.
3. **Bake the Cake:**

- Pour the batter into the prepared pan and smooth the top.
- Bake for 35-45 minutes, or until a toothpick inserted into the center comes out clean and the top is golden brown.
- Let the cake cool in the pan for 10 minutes before transferring it to a wire rack to cool completely.

4. **Prepare the Glaze:**
   - In a small bowl, whisk together the powdered sugar, milk, and vanilla extract until smooth.
   - Adjust the consistency by adding more milk or powdered sugar if needed.
5. **Decorate the Cake:**
   - Once the cake is completely cool, drizzle the glaze over the top.
   - Decorate with whole almonds and dust with powdered sugar if desired.
6. **Serve:**
   - Slice and serve the cake. The person who finds the coin or almond is said to have good luck for the year.

Enjoy your Vasilopita and the celebration of the New Year!

Galaktoboureko Cake

Ingredients

For the Custard:

- 4 cups whole milk
- 1 cup granulated sugar
- 1 cup semolina
- 4 large eggs
- 1 tsp vanilla extract
- 2 tbsp unsalted butter

For the Cake:

- 1 package (16 oz) phyllo dough, thawed
- ½ cup unsalted butter, melted

For the Syrup:

- 1 cup granulated sugar
- 1 cup water
- 1 tbsp lemon juice
- 1 tsp vanilla extract

Instructions

1. **Prepare the Custard:**
   - In a medium saucepan, heat the milk and sugar over medium heat until it begins to simmer.
   - Gradually whisk in the semolina and continue to cook, stirring constantly, until the mixture thickens and becomes smooth.
   - In a bowl, whisk the eggs and vanilla extract together.
   - Slowly temper the eggs with a bit of the hot milk mixture, then whisk the egg mixture back into the saucepan.
   - Continue to cook for another 2-3 minutes until the custard is thickened.
   - Remove from heat and stir in the butter until melted and smooth. Set aside to cool.
2. **Prepare the Phyllo Layers:**
   - Preheat your oven to 350°F (175°C). Grease a 9x13-inch baking pan.
   - Place one sheet of phyllo dough in the pan and brush with melted butter. Repeat this process, layering and buttering each sheet, until you have about 8-10 layers.
   - Spread the custard evenly over the phyllo layers.
3. **Top and Bake:**
   - Continue layering the remaining phyllo sheets over the custard, buttering each sheet as before. Aim for another 8-10 layers on top.

- Use a sharp knife to cut the top layers of phyllo into squares or diamonds.
- Bake for 45-55 minutes, or until the top is golden brown and crispy.

4. **Prepare the Syrup:**
   - While the cake is baking, combine the sugar, water, and lemon juice in a saucepan.
   - Bring to a boil, then reduce the heat and simmer for about 10 minutes until slightly thickened.
   - Remove from heat and stir in the vanilla extract. Allow the syrup to cool.

5. **Add the Syrup:**
   - Once the cake is baked and still hot, pour the cooled syrup evenly over the top.
   - Allow the cake to cool completely and absorb the syrup before cutting into squares or diamonds.

Enjoy your Galaktoboureko Cake, a scrumptious combination of creamy custard and crispy phyllo that's perfect for any special occasion!

Tiramisù Greek Style

Ingredients

For the Dessert:

- 1 cup Greek yogurt
- 1 cup mascarpone cheese
- ½ cup heavy cream
- ½ cup granulated sugar
- 1 tsp vanilla extract
- 1 cup brewed coffee, cooled
- ¼ cup brandy or liqueur (optional)
- 24-30 ladyfingers (savoiardi)
- 2 tbsp honey
- 1 tsp ground cinnamon (for dusting)

For Garnish (Optional):

- Crumbled walnuts or almonds
- Fresh mint leaves

Instructions

1. **Prepare the Cream Mixture:**
   - In a large bowl, beat the heavy cream until stiff peaks form.
   - In another bowl, combine the Greek yogurt, mascarpone cheese, granulated sugar, and vanilla extract until smooth.
   - Gently fold the whipped cream into the yogurt-mascarpone mixture until well combined.
2. **Prepare the Coffee Mixture:**
   - In a shallow dish, mix the cooled brewed coffee with the brandy or liqueur if using.
3. **Assemble the Tiramisù:**
   - Quickly dip each ladyfinger into the coffee mixture, ensuring they are coated but not soggy.
   - Arrange a layer of dipped ladyfingers in the bottom of a serving dish or individual cups.
   - Spread half of the cream mixture over the ladyfingers.
   - Repeat with another layer of dipped ladyfingers and the remaining cream mixture.
4. **Chill:**
   - Cover and refrigerate for at least 4 hours, or preferably overnight, to allow the flavors to meld and the dessert to set.
5. **Garnish and Serve:**

- - Before serving, drizzle the honey over the top and dust with ground cinnamon.
  - Optionally, sprinkle with crumbled walnuts or almonds and garnish with fresh mint leaves.

Enjoy your Tiramisù Greek Style, a creamy and refreshing take on a classic dessert!

Pasta Flora (Greek Jam Tart)

Ingredients

For the Dough:

- 2 ½ cups all-purpose flour
- 1 cup granulated sugar
- 1 cup unsalted butter, cold and cut into small pieces
- 1 large egg
- 1 tsp vanilla extract
- ½ tsp baking powder
- ¼ tsp salt

For the Filling:

- 1 cup fruit jam (apricot, strawberry, or your favorite flavor)
- Optional: 1 tbsp lemon juice (for added tang, if desired)

For the Topping:

- 1 large egg, beaten (for egg wash)
- Powdered sugar, for dusting (optional)

Instructions

1. **Prepare the Dough:**
    - In a large bowl, combine the flour, granulated sugar, baking powder, and salt.
    - Cut in the cold butter using a pastry blender or your fingers until the mixture resembles coarse crumbs.
    - In a small bowl, whisk together the egg and vanilla extract.
    - Add the egg mixture to the flour mixture and mix until the dough begins to come together. You may need to use your hands to fully combine the ingredients.
    - Form the dough into a disc, wrap it in plastic wrap, and refrigerate for at least 30 minutes.
2. **Prepare the Tart:**
    - Preheat your oven to 350°F (175°C). Grease a 9-inch tart pan with a removable bottom.
    - Remove the dough from the refrigerator and divide it into two portions: about two-thirds for the base and one-third for the lattice topping.
    - On a lightly floured surface, roll out the larger portion of dough to fit the bottom of the tart pan, including the sides. Press the dough into the pan and trim any excess. Chill the dough-lined pan while you prepare the topping.
    - Roll out the remaining dough and cut it into strips for the lattice topping.
3. **Assemble the Tart:**

- Spread the fruit jam evenly over the chilled dough in the tart pan. If using lemon juice, mix it into the jam before spreading.
- Arrange the dough strips over the jam in a lattice pattern. You can create a simple lattice by laying half of the strips in one direction and the other half in the opposite direction. Trim any excess dough from the edges.
- Brush the lattice with the beaten egg to give it a golden color.

4. **Bake the Tart:**
    - Bake in the preheated oven for 30-35 minutes, or until the crust is golden brown and the jam is bubbly.
    - Allow the tart to cool completely in the pan on a wire rack before removing the sides of the tart pan.

5. **Serve:**
    - Once cooled, dust the top with powdered sugar if desired.
    - Slice and serve. Pasta Flora is delicious on its own or paired with a cup of tea or coffee.

Enjoy your Pasta Flora, a delightful Greek jam tart that's perfect for any gathering or as a sweet treat for yourself!

Kamilaki Cake (Greek Yogurt Cake)

Ingredients

For the Cake:

- 1 ½ cups all-purpose flour
- 1 tsp baking powder
- ½ tsp baking soda
- ¼ tsp salt
- 1 cup granulated sugar
- ½ cup unsalted butter, softened
- 2 large eggs
- 1 cup plain Greek yogurt
- 1 tsp vanilla extract
- 1 tbsp lemon zest (optional)
- 2 tbsp lemon juice (optional)

For the Syrup (Optional):

- ½ cup granulated sugar
- ¼ cup water
- 1 tbsp lemon juice
- 1 tsp vanilla extract

For the Topping (Optional):

- Powdered sugar, for dusting
- Fresh berries or fruit slices

Instructions

1. **Prepare the Cake Batter:**
    - Preheat your oven to 350°F (175°C). Grease and flour a 9-inch round cake pan or a similar-sized baking dish.
    - In a medium bowl, whisk together the flour, baking powder, baking soda, and salt.
    - In a large bowl, cream the softened butter and granulated sugar until light and fluffy.
    - Beat in the eggs one at a time, making sure each is fully incorporated before adding the next.
    - Mix in the Greek yogurt, vanilla extract, and lemon zest and juice (if using).
    - Gradually add the dry ingredients to the wet ingredients, mixing until just combined.
2. **Bake the Cake:**
    - Pour the batter into the prepared pan and smooth the top.

- Bake for 25-30 minutes, or until a toothpick inserted into the center comes out clean and the top is golden brown.
- Allow the cake to cool in the pan for 10 minutes before transferring it to a wire rack to cool completely.

3. **Prepare the Syrup (Optional):**
    - In a small saucepan, combine the sugar, water, and lemon juice.
    - Bring to a boil over medium heat, stirring until the sugar is dissolved.
    - Reduce the heat and simmer for about 5 minutes, until slightly thickened.
    - Remove from heat and stir in the vanilla extract. Allow the syrup to cool.

4. **Add the Syrup (Optional):**
    - If using syrup, while the cake is still warm, brush or pour the cooled syrup evenly over the cake.
    - Let the cake absorb the syrup and cool completely.

5. **Serve:**
    - Dust with powdered sugar and top with fresh berries or fruit slices if desired.
    - Slice and enjoy your Kamilaki Cake!

This Greek Yogurt Cake is deliciously moist and subtly tangy, making it a perfect dessert for any occasion or a lovely treat with your afternoon coffee or tea. Enjoy!

Sokolatina (Chocolate Cake)

Ingredients

For the Cake:

- 1 ½ cups all-purpose flour
- 1 cup granulated sugar
- ¾ cup unsweetened cocoa powder
- 1 tsp baking powder
- 1 tsp baking soda
- ¼ tsp salt
- ½ cup unsalted butter, softened
- 2 large eggs
- 1 cup whole milk
- 1 tsp vanilla extract
- ½ cup boiling water

For the Chocolate Glaze:

- ½ cup heavy cream
- 4 oz semi-sweet chocolate, chopped
- 2 tbsp unsalted butter

Instructions

1. **Prepare the Cake Batter:**
    - Preheat your oven to 350°F (175°C). Grease and flour a 9-inch round cake pan or a similar-sized baking dish.
    - In a large bowl, sift together the flour, sugar, cocoa powder, baking powder, baking soda, and salt.
    - In another bowl, cream the softened butter until smooth. Beat in the eggs one at a time.
    - Mix in the milk and vanilla extract until well combined.
    - Gradually add the dry ingredients to the wet ingredients, mixing until just combined.
    - Stir in the boiling water until the batter is smooth and well combined. The batter will be thin.
2. **Bake the Cake:**
    - Pour the batter into the prepared pan and smooth the top.
    - Bake for 30-35 minutes, or until a toothpick inserted into the center comes out clean and the cake is set.
    - Allow the cake to cool in the pan for 10 minutes before transferring it to a wire rack to cool completely.
3. **Prepare the Chocolate Glaze:**

- In a small saucepan, heat the heavy cream over medium heat until it begins to simmer. Do not let it boil.
- Remove from heat and add the chopped chocolate. Stir until the chocolate is completely melted and the mixture is smooth.
- Stir in the butter until fully incorporated and the glaze is shiny.

4. **Glaze the Cake:**
   - Once the cake has cooled completely, place it on a serving plate.
   - Pour the chocolate glaze over the cake, spreading it evenly with a spatula.
   - Allow the glaze to set before slicing.

5. **Serve:**
   - Slice and serve your rich and decadent Sokolatina. It pairs beautifully with a dollop of whipped cream or a scoop of vanilla ice cream.

Enjoy this delicious Greek chocolate cake that's sure to satisfy any chocolate craving!

Rizogalo Cake (Rice Pudding Cake)

Ingredients

For the Rice Pudding Layer:

- 1 cup short-grain rice (such as Arborio)
- 4 cups whole milk
- ½ cup granulated sugar
- 1 tsp vanilla extract
- 1 tsp ground cinnamon
- 1 tbsp cornstarch (optional, for thickening)

For the Cake Layer:

- 1 cup all-purpose flour
- 1 tsp baking powder
- ¼ tsp salt
- ½ cup unsalted butter, softened
- ¾ cup granulated sugar
- 2 large eggs
- ½ cup milk
- 1 tsp vanilla extract

For the Topping (Optional):

- Ground cinnamon
- Powdered sugar

Instructions

1. **Prepare the Rice Pudding:**
    - Rinse the rice under cold water.
    - In a medium saucepan, combine the rice, milk, and sugar. Bring to a simmer over medium heat, stirring frequently.
    - Reduce the heat and cook for about 20-25 minutes, stirring occasionally, until the rice is tender and the mixture has thickened.
    - Stir in the vanilla extract and ground cinnamon.
    - If you prefer a thicker pudding, dissolve the cornstarch in a little milk and stir it into the mixture, cooking for an additional 2-3 minutes until thickened. Remove from heat and let cool.
2. **Prepare the Cake Batter:**
    - Preheat your oven to 350°F (175°C). Grease and flour an 8-inch round or square cake pan.
    - In a medium bowl, whisk together the flour, baking powder, and salt.

- In a large bowl, cream the softened butter and granulated sugar until light and fluffy.
- Beat in the eggs one at a time.
- Mix in the milk and vanilla extract until well combined.
- Gradually add the dry ingredients to the wet ingredients, mixing until just combined.

3. **Assemble and Bake:**
   - Pour the cake batter into the prepared pan and smooth the top.
   - Spoon the rice pudding evenly over the cake batter, spreading it out gently.
   - Bake for 40-45 minutes, or until the cake layer is golden and a toothpick inserted into the cake part comes out clean.

4. **Cool and Serve:**
   - Allow the cake to cool in the pan for about 10 minutes before transferring to a wire rack to cool completely.
   - Once cool, dust with ground cinnamon and powdered sugar if desired.

5. **Serve:**
   - Slice and enjoy your Rizogalo Cake as a unique twist on traditional rice pudding.

This cake combines the creamy texture of rice pudding with a soft cake base, offering a comforting and delicious dessert. Enjoy!

Spoon Sweet Cake

Ingredients

For the Cake:

- 1 ½ cups all-purpose flour
- 1 tsp baking powder
- ¼ tsp salt
- ½ cup unsalted butter, softened
- 1 cup granulated sugar
- 3 large eggs
- 1 cup Greek yogurt
- 1 tsp vanilla extract
- ¼ cup milk

For the Spoon Sweet Topping:

- 1 cup spoon sweet (any flavor, such as cherry, peach, or quince), chopped if large pieces
- ¼ cup chopped nuts (optional, such as walnuts or almonds)

For the Glaze (Optional):

- 1 cup powdered sugar
- 2-3 tbsp lemon juice or milk

Instructions

1. **Prepare the Cake Batter:**
    - Preheat your oven to 350°F (175°C). Grease and flour a 9-inch round cake pan or a similar-sized baking dish.
    - In a medium bowl, whisk together the flour, baking powder, and salt.
    - In a large bowl, cream the softened butter and granulated sugar until light and fluffy.
    - Beat in the eggs one at a time.
    - Mix in the Greek yogurt, vanilla extract, and milk until well combined.
    - Gradually add the dry ingredients to the wet ingredients, mixing until just combined.
2. **Bake the Cake:**
    - Pour the batter into the prepared pan and smooth the top.
    - Bake for 30-35 minutes, or until a toothpick inserted into the center comes out clean and the cake is golden brown.
    - Allow the cake to cool in the pan for 10 minutes before transferring it to a wire rack to cool completely.
3. **Prepare the Spoon Sweet Topping:**

- While the cake is cooling, chop the spoon sweet into smaller pieces if necessary. If using a spoon sweet with syrup, you may want to drain it slightly to avoid excess moisture on the cake.
4. **Assemble the Cake:**
    - Once the cake is completely cooled, spread or spoon the chopped spoon sweet evenly over the top of the cake.
    - If desired, sprinkle with chopped nuts for added texture and flavor.
5. **Prepare the Glaze (Optional):**
    - In a small bowl, whisk together the powdered sugar and lemon juice or milk until smooth and pourable.
    - Drizzle the glaze over the spoon sweet topping.
6. **Serve:**
    - Slice and serve the cake. Enjoy the combination of moist cake and sweet, flavorful preserves!

This Spoon Sweet Cake is a wonderful way to incorporate the flavors of traditional Greek spoon sweets into a cake, offering a unique and delightful dessert experience.

Chocolatina

Ingredients

For the Cake:

- 1 ½ cups all-purpose flour
- 1 cup granulated sugar
- ¾ cup unsweetened cocoa powder
- 1 tsp baking powder
- 1 tsp baking soda
- ¼ tsp salt
- ½ cup unsalted butter, melted
- 2 large eggs
- 1 cup buttermilk (or regular milk)
- 1 tsp vanilla extract
- ½ cup boiling water

For the Chocolate Glaze:

- ½ cup heavy cream
- 4 oz semi-sweet chocolate, chopped
- 2 tbsp unsalted butter

For the Topping (Optional):

- Whipped cream
- Fresh berries or fruit slices
- Shaved chocolate or cocoa powder

Instructions

1. **Prepare the Cake Batter:**
    - Preheat your oven to 350°F (175°C). Grease and flour a 9-inch round cake pan or a similar-sized baking dish.
    - In a large bowl, sift together the flour, sugar, cocoa powder, baking powder, baking soda, and salt.
    - In another bowl, whisk together the melted butter, eggs, buttermilk, and vanilla extract.
    - Gradually add the wet ingredients to the dry ingredients, mixing until just combined.
    - Stir in the boiling water until the batter is smooth. The batter will be thin, but this is normal.
2. **Bake the Cake:**
    - Pour the batter into the prepared pan and smooth the top.

- Bake for 30-35 minutes, or until a toothpick inserted into the center comes out clean and the cake is set.
- Allow the cake to cool in the pan for 10 minutes before transferring it to a wire rack to cool completely.

3. **Prepare the Chocolate Glaze:**
   - In a small saucepan, heat the heavy cream over medium heat until it begins to simmer. Do not let it boil.
   - Remove from heat and add the chopped chocolate. Let it sit for a minute, then stir until the chocolate is completely melted and the mixture is smooth.
   - Stir in the butter until fully incorporated and the glaze is shiny.
4. **Glaze the Cake:**
   - Once the cake has cooled completely, place it on a serving plate.
   - Pour the chocolate glaze over the top of the cake, spreading it evenly with a spatula.
   - Allow the glaze to set before slicing.
5. **Serve:**
   - Slice and serve your Chocolatina. Garnish with whipped cream, fresh berries, or shaved chocolate if desired.

Enjoy this rich and delicious Greek chocolate cake that's sure to impress your guests or satisfy your chocolate cravings!

Panzaroti Cake

Ingredients

For the Cake:

- 1 ½ cups all-purpose flour
- 1 cup granulated sugar
- 1 tsp baking powder
- ½ tsp baking soda
- ¼ tsp salt
- ½ cup unsalted butter, softened
- 2 large eggs
- 1 cup plain Greek yogurt
- 1 tsp vanilla extract
- ¼ cup milk
- 1 cup fruit preserves or jam (such as apricot, peach, or cherry), slightly warmed to make spreading easier

For the Topping (Optional):

- Powdered sugar, for dusting
- Fresh fruit or berries

Instructions

1. **Prepare the Cake Batter:**
    - Preheat your oven to 350°F (175°C). Grease and flour a 9-inch round or square cake pan.
    - In a medium bowl, whisk together the flour, baking powder, baking soda, and salt.
    - In a large bowl, cream the softened butter and granulated sugar until light and fluffy.
    - Beat in the eggs one at a time, ensuring each is fully incorporated before adding the next.
    - Mix in the Greek yogurt and vanilla extract until well combined.
    - Gradually add the dry ingredients to the wet ingredients, mixing until just combined.
    - Stir in the milk until the batter is smooth.
2. **Assemble the Cake:**
    - Pour about half of the cake batter into the prepared pan and spread it evenly.
    - Spoon the fruit preserves over the batter, spreading it out evenly but leaving a small border around the edges to prevent leakage.
    - Gently spread the remaining batter over the fruit preserves, covering it completely.
3. **Bake the Cake:**

- Bake in the preheated oven for 30-35 minutes, or until a toothpick inserted into the center of the cake comes out clean and the top is golden brown.
- Allow the cake to cool in the pan for about 10 minutes before transferring it to a wire rack to cool completely.
4. **Serve:**
    - Once the cake has cooled, dust the top with powdered sugar if desired.
    - Optionally, garnish with fresh fruit or berries for added color and flavor.
    - Slice and enjoy your Panzaroti Cake, which pairs beautifully with a cup of tea or coffee.

This Panzaroti Cake is a wonderful blend of moist cake and fruity sweetness, making it a delightful dessert for any occasion. Enjoy!

Amoita Cake

Ingredients:

- 1 cup all-purpose flour
- 1 cup sugar
- 1/2 cup Greek yogurt
- 1/2 cup olive oil
- 3 large eggs
- 1 tsp baking powder
- 1/2 tsp baking soda
- 1 tsp vanilla extract
- 1/2 cup chopped nuts (optional)
- Zest of 1 lemon

Instructions:

1. Preheat your oven to 350°F (175°C). Grease and flour a cake pan.
2. In a bowl, mix flour, baking powder, baking soda, and lemon zest.
3. In another bowl, whisk eggs and sugar until light and fluffy.
4. Add yogurt, olive oil, and vanilla extract to the egg mixture.
5. Gradually incorporate the dry ingredients into the wet mixture.
6. Fold in nuts if using.
7. Pour the batter into the prepared pan and bake for 30-35 minutes, or until a toothpick inserted in the center comes out clean.
8. Let it cool before serving.

This cake should give you a delightful taste of Greek baking!

Kourabiedes Cake

Ingredients:

- 1 cup unsalted butter, softened
- 1/2 cup powdered sugar, plus extra for dusting
- 1 egg yolk
- 1 tsp vanilla extract
- 1/4 cup finely chopped almonds (optional, but traditional)
- 2 1/4 cups all-purpose flour
- 1/4 tsp baking powder
- A pinch of salt
- 1/4 tsp rose water (optional, for a more traditional flavor)

Instructions:

1. **Preheat Oven:** Preheat your oven to 350°F (175°C). Line a baking sheet with parchment paper.
2. **Cream Butter and Sugar:** In a large bowl, beat the softened butter and 1/2 cup powdered sugar until light and fluffy.
3. **Add Egg and Vanilla:** Mix in the egg yolk and vanilla extract. If using, add rose water at this stage.
4. **Combine Dry Ingredients:** In another bowl, whisk together the flour, baking powder, and salt. Gradually add this mixture to the butter mixture, mixing until combined.
5. **Incorporate Nuts:** Fold in the chopped almonds, if using.
6. **Shape Cookies:** Take small amounts of dough and roll them into balls (about 1 inch in diameter). Place them on the prepared baking sheet and gently flatten them with the palm of your hand or the bottom of a glass. You can also shape them into crescent moons or other forms if you prefer.
7. **Bake:** Bake for 15-20 minutes, or until the edges are lightly golden. The cookies should be set but still pale in color.
8. **Cool and Dust:** Let the cookies cool on a wire rack. Once cool, generously dust them with powdered sugar.

Kourabiedes are often enjoyed around the holidays and are perfect for sharing with family and friends. Enjoy your baking!

Kremasti Cake

Ingredients:

- 1 cup sugar
- 1 cup butter
- 4 large eggs
- 1 1/2 cups flour
- 1/2 cup milk
- 1 tsp vanilla extract
- 1 tsp baking powder
- 1/4 tsp salt

Instructions:

1. Preheat your oven to 350°F (175°C). Grease and flour a cake pan.
2. Cream together sugar and butter until light and fluffy.
3. Beat in eggs one at a time.
4. Mix in vanilla extract.
5. In another bowl, whisk together flour, baking powder, and salt.
6. Gradually add the dry ingredients to the butter mixture, alternating with milk.
7. Pour batter into the prepared pan and bake for 30-35 minutes, or until a toothpick inserted comes out clean.
8. Let cool before serving.

Enjoy your cake!

Sour Cherry Cake

Ingredients:

- 1 1/2 cups fresh or frozen sour cherries (pitted)
- 1 1/2 cups all-purpose flour
- 1 cup granulated sugar
- 1/2 cup unsalted butter, softened
- 2 large eggs
- 1/2 cup milk
- 1 tsp vanilla extract
- 2 tsp baking powder
- 1/4 tsp salt
- Powdered sugar, for dusting (optional)

Instructions:

1. **Prepare the Oven and Pan:**
   - Preheat your oven to 350°F (175°C).
   - Grease and flour an 8-inch round cake pan or line it with parchment paper.
2. **Prepare the Cherries:**
   - If using frozen cherries, thaw them and drain excess liquid. Pat them dry with a paper towel. If using fresh cherries, pit and halve them.
3. **Mix the Dry Ingredients:**
   - In a medium bowl, whisk together the flour, baking powder, and salt. Set aside.
4. **Cream the Butter and Sugar:**
   - In a large mixing bowl, cream the softened butter and granulated sugar until light and fluffy.
5. **Add Eggs and Vanilla:**
   - Beat in the eggs one at a time, mixing well after each addition. Stir in the vanilla extract.
6. **Combine Wet and Dry Ingredients:**
   - Gradually add the flour mixture to the butter mixture, alternating with the milk. Begin and end with the flour mixture. Mix until just combined; do not overmix.
7. **Fold in the Cherries:**
   - Gently fold the sour cherries into the batter, distributing them evenly.
8. **Bake the Cake:**
   - Pour the batter into the prepared cake pan and smooth the top.
   - Bake for 35-40 minutes, or until a toothpick inserted into the center comes out clean.
9. **Cool and Serve:**
   - Allow the cake to cool in the pan for about 10 minutes before transferring it to a wire rack to cool completely.
   - Dust with powdered sugar before serving, if desired.

Enjoy your Sour Cherry Cake with a cup of tea or coffee!

Almond Cake (Amygdalopita)

Ingredients:

- 2 cups ground almonds
- 1 cup granulated sugar
- 4 large eggs
- 1/2 cup unsalted butter, melted
- 1/2 tsp baking powder
- 1/4 tsp salt
- 1 tsp vanilla extract
- Powdered sugar for dusting (optional)

Instructions:

1. **Preheat Oven:**
   - Preheat your oven to 350°F (175°C). Grease and flour a 9-inch round cake pan or line it with parchment paper.
2. **Prepare the Batter:**
   - In a large bowl, combine the ground almonds, sugar, baking powder, and salt.
   - In another bowl, whisk the eggs until frothy. Mix in the melted butter and vanilla extract.
   - Gradually add the egg mixture to the almond mixture, stirring until well combined.
3. **Bake the Cake:**
   - Pour the batter into the prepared pan and smooth the top.
   - Bake for 30-35 minutes, or until a toothpick inserted into the center comes out clean.
4. **Cool and Serve:**
   - Allow the cake to cool in the pan for 10 minutes before transferring it to a wire rack to cool completely.
   - Dust with powdered sugar before serving, if desired.

Enjoy your Amygdalopita with a cup of coffee or tea!

Baklava Cheesecake

Ingredients:

For the Crust:

- 1 1/2 cups crushed graham crackers
- 1/2 cup chopped walnuts or almonds (optional, for added texture)
- 1/4 cup granulated sugar
- 1/2 cup unsalted butter, melted

For the Baklava Filling:

- 1 cup chopped walnuts or almonds
- 1/2 cup granulated sugar
- 1/2 tsp ground cinnamon
- 1/4 cup unsalted butter, melted

For the Cheesecake Filling:

- 4 (8 oz each) packages cream cheese, softened
- 1 cup granulated sugar
- 1 tsp vanilla extract
- 4 large eggs
- 1 cup sour cream
- 1/2 cup heavy cream

For the Syrup:

- 1 cup water
- 1 cup granulated sugar
- 1/2 cup honey
- 1/2 tsp vanilla extract
- 1/2 tsp lemon juice

Instructions:

1. **Prepare the Crust:**
    - Preheat your oven to 325°F (165°C).
    - In a medium bowl, combine crushed graham crackers, chopped nuts (if using), granulated sugar, and melted butter.
    - Press the mixture into the bottom of a 9-inch springform pan to form an even layer. Bake for 10 minutes. Remove from the oven and set aside.
2. **Prepare the Baklava Filling:**
    - In a small bowl, mix chopped nuts, granulated sugar, ground cinnamon, and melted butter. Set aside.

3. **Prepare the Cheesecake Filling:**
    - In a large mixing bowl, beat the cream cheese and sugar until smooth and creamy.
    - Add the vanilla extract and beat until combined.
    - Add the eggs one at a time, mixing on low speed after each addition. Be careful not to overmix.
    - Mix in the sour cream and heavy cream until smooth.
4. **Assemble the Cheesecake:**
    - Pour half of the cheesecake batter over the prepared crust.
    - Sprinkle the baklava filling evenly over the batter.
    - Pour the remaining cheesecake batter over the baklava filling and smooth the top.
5. **Bake the Cheesecake:**
    - Bake for 55-65 minutes, or until the edges are set but the center is still slightly jiggly. Turn off the oven and let the cheesecake cool in the oven with the door slightly open for about 1 hour.
6. **Prepare the Syrup:**
    - While the cheesecake is cooling, combine water, granulated sugar, honey, vanilla extract, and lemon juice in a saucepan.
    - Bring to a boil over medium heat, then reduce the heat and simmer for about 10 minutes, or until the syrup thickens slightly. Let it cool.
7. **Chill the Cheesecake:**
    - After the cheesecake has cooled, refrigerate it for at least 4 hours or overnight.
8. **Serve:**
    - Drizzle the cooled syrup over the cheesecake before serving.

Enjoy your Baklava Cheesecake with its rich layers of flavor and delightful sweetness!

Lemon Phyllo Cake

Ingredients:

For the Phyllo Layers:

- 1 package (16 oz) phyllo dough, thawed
- 1 cup unsalted butter, melted

For the Lemon Filling:

- 1 cup granulated sugar
- 1/2 cup lemon juice (freshly squeezed)
- 4 large eggs
- 1/2 cup all-purpose flour
- 1/4 cup milk
- 1/4 tsp salt
- 1 tbsp lemon zest

For the Syrup (Optional):

- 1/2 cup granulated sugar
- 1/2 cup water
- 2 tbsp lemon juice
- 1 tsp vanilla extract

Instructions:

1. **Preheat Oven:**
   - Preheat your oven to 350°F (175°C). Grease a 9x13-inch baking dish or a similar-sized pan.
2. **Prepare the Phyllo Layers:**
   - Place a sheet of phyllo dough in the prepared pan and brush with melted butter. Repeat with additional sheets, brushing each with butter, until you have about 10 layers of phyllo.
   - Keep the remaining phyllo sheets covered with a damp towel to prevent them from drying out.
3. **Prepare the Lemon Filling:**
   - In a large bowl, whisk together the granulated sugar, lemon juice, and eggs until well combined.
   - Stir in the flour, milk, salt, and lemon zest until smooth.
4. **Assemble the Cake:**
   - Pour the lemon filling over the layered phyllo dough in the pan.
   - Continue layering the remaining phyllo sheets on top of the filling, brushing each sheet with melted butter, until you have used up all the phyllo. Finish with a final layer of butter-brushed phyllo.

5. **Bake the Cake:**
   - Bake for 45-50 minutes, or until the phyllo is golden brown and the lemon filling is set. A knife inserted into the center should come out clean.
6. **Prepare the Syrup (Optional):**
   - While the cake is baking, combine granulated sugar, water, lemon juice, and vanilla extract in a small saucepan.
   - Bring to a boil, then reduce the heat and simmer for about 10 minutes, or until the syrup has thickened slightly. Let it cool.
7. **Cool and Serve:**
   - Allow the cake to cool completely before cutting into squares.
   - If using the syrup, drizzle it over the cooled cake before serving.

Enjoy your Lemon Phyllo Cake with its crisp layers and zesty lemon flavor!

Zacharopita (Sweet Cake)

Ingredients:

For the Cake:

- 1 1/2 cups all-purpose flour
- 1 cup granulated sugar
- 1 cup chopped nuts (such as walnuts or almonds)
- 1/2 cup unsalted butter, melted
- 2 large eggs
- 1 cup milk
- 1 tsp baking powder
- 1/2 tsp baking soda
- 1/2 tsp ground cinnamon
- 1/4 tsp ground cloves
- 1/4 tsp salt
- 1 tsp vanilla extract

For the Syrup:

- 1 cup granulated sugar
- 1 cup water
- 1/2 cup honey
- 1/2 tsp vanilla extract
- 1/2 tsp lemon juice

Instructions:

1. **Preheat Oven:**
    - Preheat your oven to 350°F (175°C). Grease and flour a 9-inch round or square cake pan.
2. **Prepare the Cake Batter:**
    - In a large bowl, whisk together the flour, baking powder, baking soda, cinnamon, cloves, and salt.
    - In another bowl, beat the eggs and sugar until light and fluffy. Stir in the melted butter and vanilla extract.
    - Gradually add the flour mixture to the egg mixture, alternating with the milk, until well combined.
    - Fold in the chopped nuts.
3. **Bake the Cake:**
    - Pour the batter into the prepared cake pan and smooth the top.
    - Bake for 35-40 minutes, or until a toothpick inserted into the center comes out clean.
4. **Prepare the Syrup:**

- While the cake is baking, combine granulated sugar, water, honey, vanilla extract, and lemon juice in a small saucepan.
- Bring to a boil over medium heat, then reduce the heat and simmer for about 10 minutes, or until the syrup thickens slightly. Allow it to cool.

5. **Assemble the Cake:**
    - Once the cake is done baking, let it cool in the pan for about 10 minutes before transferring it to a wire rack.
    - While the cake is still warm, pour the cooled syrup evenly over the cake. Let the cake absorb the syrup and cool completely before serving.

Enjoy your Zacharopita with a cup of coffee or tea! This cake is perfect for special occasions or as a sweet treat anytime.

Chocolatopita

Ingredients:

For the Cake:

- 1 cup all-purpose flour
- 1 cup granulated sugar
- 1/2 cup unsweetened cocoa powder
- 1 tsp baking powder
- 1/2 tsp baking soda
- 1/4 tsp salt
- 1/2 cup vegetable oil
- 1/2 cup milk
- 2 large eggs
- 1 tsp vanilla extract
- 1/2 cup boiling water

For the Chocolate Ganache (Optional):

- 1 cup heavy cream
- 6 oz semi-sweet chocolate, chopped
- 1 tbsp unsalted butter

Instructions:

1. **Preheat Oven:**
    - Preheat your oven to 350°F (175°C). Grease and flour a 9-inch round cake pan or line it with parchment paper.
2. **Prepare the Cake Batter:**
    - In a large bowl, sift together the flour, sugar, cocoa powder, baking powder, baking soda, and salt.
    - In another bowl, whisk together the vegetable oil, milk, eggs, and vanilla extract.
    - Gradually add the wet ingredients to the dry ingredients, mixing until just combined.
    - Stir in the boiling water until the batter is smooth and well combined (the batter will be thin).
3. **Bake the Cake:**
    - Pour the batter into the prepared cake pan.
    - Bake for 30-35 minutes, or until a toothpick inserted into the center comes out clean.
    - Allow the cake to cool in the pan for 10 minutes before transferring it to a wire rack to cool completely.
4. **Prepare the Ganache (Optional):**
    - Heat the heavy cream in a saucepan over medium heat until it begins to simmer.

- Remove from heat and add the chopped chocolate. Let it sit for 5 minutes, then stir until smooth.
    - Stir in the butter until fully melted and incorporated.
    - Let the ganache cool slightly before spreading it over the cooled cake.
5. **Assemble the Cake:**
    - Once the cake has cooled completely, spread the chocolate ganache evenly over the top. You can also frost the sides if you prefer.
6. **Serve:**
    - Let the ganache set for about 30 minutes before slicing and serving.

Enjoy your Chocolatopita with a glass of milk or a cup of coffee! This rich chocolate cake is perfect for any chocolate lover.

Kokkinopita (Red Cake)

Ingredients:

For the Cake:

- 1 cup all-purpose flour
- 1 cup granulated sugar
- 1/2 cup unsweetened cocoa powder
- 1 tsp baking powder
- 1/2 tsp baking soda
- 1/4 tsp salt
- 1/2 cup vegetable oil
- 1/2 cup pomegranate juice (or beet juice for a different flavor)
- 2 large eggs
- 1 tsp vanilla extract
- 1/2 cup sour cream

For the Glaze (Optional):

- 1/2 cup pomegranate juice
- 1/4 cup granulated sugar

Instructions:

1. **Preheat Oven:**
    - Preheat your oven to 350°F (175°C). Grease and flour a 9-inch round cake pan or line it with parchment paper.
2. **Prepare the Cake Batter:**
    - In a large bowl, sift together the flour, sugar, cocoa powder, baking powder, baking soda, and salt.
    - In another bowl, whisk together the vegetable oil, pomegranate juice, eggs, vanilla extract, and sour cream until well combined.
    - Gradually add the wet ingredients to the dry ingredients, mixing until just combined.
3. **Bake the Cake:**
    - Pour the batter into the prepared cake pan.
    - Bake for 30-35 minutes, or until a toothpick inserted into the center comes out clean.
    - Allow the cake to cool in the pan for 10 minutes before transferring it to a wire rack to cool completely.
4. **Prepare the Glaze (Optional):**
    - In a small saucepan, combine pomegranate juice and sugar.
    - Bring to a boil over medium heat, then reduce the heat and simmer until the mixture thickens slightly, about 5-7 minutes. Let it cool before using.

5. **Assemble the Cake:**
    - Once the cake has cooled, drizzle the pomegranate glaze over the top if using.

Enjoy your Kokkinopita with its unique red color and deliciously sweet flavor!

Phyllo-Wrapped Pumpkin Cake

Ingredients:

For the Pumpkin Filling:

- 1 can (15 oz) pumpkin puree
- 1/2 cup granulated sugar
- 1/2 cup brown sugar, packed
- 2 large eggs
- 1/2 cup heavy cream
- 1/2 tsp ground cinnamon
- 1/4 tsp ground nutmeg
- 1/4 tsp ground ginger
- 1/4 tsp ground cloves
- 1/4 tsp salt

For the Phyllo Dough:

- 1 package (16 oz) phyllo dough, thawed
- 1/2 cup unsalted butter, melted
- 1/2 cup chopped nuts (optional, for added texture)

Instructions:

1. **Preheat Oven:**
   - Preheat your oven to 350°F (175°C). Grease a 9-inch round or square baking dish.
2. **Prepare the Pumpkin Filling:**
   - In a large bowl, whisk together pumpkin puree, granulated sugar, brown sugar, eggs, heavy cream, cinnamon, nutmeg, ginger, cloves, and salt until smooth.
3. **Prepare the Phyllo Dough:**
   - Unroll the phyllo dough and cover with a damp cloth to prevent drying out.
   - Brush a sheet of phyllo dough with melted butter, then place another sheet on top. Continue layering and buttering the sheets until you have about 8-10 layers.
   - Sprinkle a layer of chopped nuts between some of the layers if using.
4. **Assemble the Cake:**
   - Pour the pumpkin filling into the prepared baking dish.
   - Carefully place the layered phyllo dough over the pumpkin filling, tucking the edges into the sides of the dish. Brush the top with additional melted butter.
5. **Bake the Cake:**
   - Bake for 50-60 minutes, or until the phyllo is golden brown and the pumpkin filling is set. A knife inserted into the center should come out clean.
6. **Cool and Serve:**
   - Allow the cake to cool before slicing into pieces.

Enjoy your Phyllo-Wrapped Pumpkin Cake, a perfect blend of crisp phyllo and creamy pumpkin!

Pavlova Greek Style

Ingredients:

For the Meringue Base:

- 4 large egg whites
- 1 cup granulated sugar
- 1 tsp cornstarch
- 1 tsp white vinegar
- 1/2 tsp vanilla extract

For the Topping:

- 1 cup Greek yogurt (full-fat or strained for a thicker consistency)
- 2-3 tbsp honey (or to taste)
- 1 tsp vanilla extract
- Fresh fruit (such as berries, sliced peaches, or kiwi)
- Fresh mint leaves (for garnish, optional)

Instructions:

1. **Prepare the Meringue:**
   - Preheat your oven to 275°F (135°C). Line a baking sheet with parchment paper.
   - In a large, clean mixing bowl, beat the egg whites with an electric mixer until soft peaks form.
   - Gradually add the granulated sugar, a tablespoon at a time, continuing to beat until stiff, glossy peaks form.
   - Gently fold in the cornstarch, vinegar, and vanilla extract until just combined.
   - Spoon the meringue onto the prepared baking sheet, forming a circular shape with a slight indentation in the center to hold the toppings later.
2. **Bake the Meringue:**
   - Bake for 1 hour to 1 hour 15 minutes, or until the meringue is crisp and dry on the outside but still slightly soft in the center. The exterior should be a pale, off-white color.
   - Turn off the oven and let the meringue cool in the oven with the door slightly ajar. This helps prevent cracking.
3. **Prepare the Topping:**
   - In a medium bowl, mix the Greek yogurt with honey and vanilla extract until smooth and well combined.
   - Chill the yogurt mixture in the refrigerator until ready to use.
4. **Assemble the Pavlova:**
   - Once the meringue has completely cooled, carefully transfer it to a serving platter.

- Spoon the Greek yogurt mixture into the center of the meringue, spreading it out slightly but leaving a border of meringue exposed.
- Top with fresh fruit and garnish with mint leaves, if desired.

5. **Serve:**
   - Serve the pavlova immediately after assembling for the best texture, as the meringue can start to soften if left for too long.

Enjoy your Greek-Style Pavlova, a refreshing and elegant dessert that combines the light, airy texture of meringue with creamy Greek yogurt and fresh fruit!

Cheese Pie Cake

Ingredients:

For the Cake:

- 1 1/2 cups all-purpose flour
- 1/2 cup granulated sugar
- 1 tsp baking powder
- 1/2 tsp baking soda
- 1/4 tsp salt
- 1/2 cup unsalted butter, softened
- 1/2 cup milk
- 2 large eggs
- 1 tsp vanilla extract

For the Cheese Filling:

- 1 1/2 cups ricotta cheese (or Greek feta cheese, crumbled)
- 1 cup shredded mozzarella cheese
- 1/2 cup grated Parmesan cheese
- 2 large eggs
- 1/4 cup chopped fresh parsley (optional)
- 1/2 tsp black pepper

For the Topping (Optional):

- 1 egg, beaten (for brushing the top)
- Sesame seeds or poppy seeds (for garnish)

Instructions:

1. **Preheat Oven:**
    - Preheat your oven to 350°F (175°C). Grease and flour a 9-inch round or square baking dish.
2. **Prepare the Cake Batter:**
    - In a medium bowl, whisk together flour, sugar, baking powder, baking soda, and salt.
    - In a large bowl, beat the softened butter until creamy. Add the milk, eggs, and vanilla extract, and mix well.
    - Gradually add the dry ingredients to the wet ingredients, mixing until just combined.
3. **Prepare the Cheese Filling:**
    - In a separate bowl, combine ricotta cheese, mozzarella cheese, Parmesan cheese, eggs, parsley (if using), and black pepper. Mix until smooth and well combined.

4. **Assemble the Cake:**
    - Pour half of the cake batter into the prepared baking dish and spread it evenly.
    - Spoon the cheese filling over the batter, spreading it out evenly.
    - Top with the remaining cake batter, smoothing it over the cheese filling.
5. **Add Topping (Optional):**
    - Brush the top of the cake with the beaten egg. Sprinkle with sesame seeds or poppy seeds if desired.
6. **Bake the Cake:**
    - Bake for 35-45 minutes, or until a toothpick inserted into the center comes out clean and the top is golden brown.
7. **Cool and Serve:**
    - Allow the cake to cool in the pan for about 10 minutes before transferring it to a wire rack to cool completely.
    - Cut into squares or wedges and serve warm or at room temperature.

This Cheese Pie Cake is a savory, cheesy treat that's sure to be a hit at any gathering. Enjoy!

Greek Apple Cake

Ingredients:

For the Cake:

- 2 cups all-purpose flour
- 1 1/2 tsp baking powder
- 1/2 tsp baking soda
- 1/4 tsp salt
- 1 tsp ground cinnamon
- 1/4 tsp ground cloves
- 1/2 cup unsalted butter, softened
- 1 cup granulated sugar
- 2 large eggs
- 1/2 cup Greek yogurt or sour cream
- 1 tsp vanilla extract
- 2 medium apples, peeled, cored, and diced (about 2 cups)
- 1/2 cup chopped walnuts or pecans (optional)

For the Topping:

- 1/4 cup granulated sugar
- 1 tsp ground cinnamon
- 1 tbsp unsalted butter, melted

Instructions:

1. **Preheat Oven:**
    - Preheat your oven to 350°F (175°C). Grease and flour a 9-inch round or square cake pan, or line it with parchment paper.
2. **Prepare the Dry Ingredients:**
    - In a medium bowl, whisk together the flour, baking powder, baking soda, salt, cinnamon, and cloves. Set aside.
3. **Cream the Butter and Sugar:**
    - In a large bowl, beat the softened butter and granulated sugar until light and fluffy.
    - Beat in the eggs one at a time, mixing well after each addition.
4. **Combine Wet Ingredients:**
    - Mix in the Greek yogurt (or sour cream) and vanilla extract until well combined.
5. **Combine Wet and Dry Ingredients:**
    - Gradually add the dry ingredients to the wet ingredients, mixing until just combined. The batter will be thick.
6. **Add Apples and Nuts:**
    - Fold in the diced apples and chopped nuts (if using).

7. **Assemble the Cake:**
   - Pour the batter into the prepared cake pan and spread it evenly.
8. **Prepare the Topping:**
   - In a small bowl, mix together the granulated sugar and ground cinnamon. Sprinkle this mixture evenly over the top of the batter.
   - Drizzle the melted butter over the top of the cake.
9. **Bake the Cake:**
   - Bake for 45-50 minutes, or until a toothpick inserted into the center comes out clean and the top is golden brown.
10. **Cool and Serve:**
    - Allow the cake to cool in the pan for about 10 minutes before transferring it to a wire rack to cool completely.
    - Serve warm or at room temperature. You can dust it with powdered sugar before serving if desired.

Enjoy your Greek Apple Cake with a cup of coffee or tea! Its warm spices and tender apple chunks make it a comforting and delicious treat.

Nuts and Honey Cake

Ingredients:

For the Cake:

- 1 cup all-purpose flour
- 1 cup ground nuts (such as walnuts, almonds, or a mix)
- 1/2 cup granulated sugar
- 1/2 cup unsalted butter, softened
- 3 large eggs
- 1/2 cup Greek yogurt or sour cream
- 1 tsp baking powder
- 1/2 tsp baking soda
- 1/2 tsp vanilla extract
- 1/2 tsp ground cinnamon (optional)
- 1/4 tsp salt

For the Honey Syrup:

- 1 cup honey
- 1/2 cup water
- 1/2 cup granulated sugar
- 1/2 tsp vanilla extract
- 1/2 tsp lemon juice (optional)

Instructions:

1. **Preheat Oven:**
   - Preheat your oven to 350°F (175°C). Grease and flour a 9-inch round or square cake pan, or line it with parchment paper.
2. **Prepare the Cake Batter:**
   - In a medium bowl, whisk together the flour, baking powder, baking soda, salt, and ground cinnamon (if using). Set aside.
   - In a large bowl, beat the softened butter and granulated sugar until light and fluffy.
   - Beat in the eggs one at a time, mixing well after each addition.
   - Mix in the Greek yogurt (or sour cream) and vanilla extract until smooth.
   - Gradually add the dry ingredients to the wet ingredients, mixing until just combined.
   - Fold in the ground nuts.
3. **Bake the Cake:**
   - Pour the batter into the prepared cake pan and smooth the top.
   - Bake for 35-40 minutes, or until a toothpick inserted into the center comes out clean and the cake is golden brown.

4. **Prepare the Honey Syrup:**
   - While the cake is baking, combine honey, water, and granulated sugar in a small saucepan.
   - Bring to a boil over medium heat, then reduce the heat and simmer for about 10 minutes, or until the syrup thickens slightly. Stir in the vanilla extract and lemon juice (if using). Let it cool.
5. **Assemble the Cake:**
   - Once the cake is baked, allow it to cool in the pan for about 10 minutes.
   - Transfer the cake to a wire rack set over a baking sheet or parchment paper (to catch any drips).
   - While the cake is still warm, pour the cooled honey syrup evenly over the cake, allowing it to soak in.
6. **Cool and Serve:**
   - Let the cake cool completely before slicing and serving.

Enjoy your Nuts and Honey Cake with its rich flavors and delightful sweetness! It pairs beautifully with a cup of coffee or tea.

Honey Cake with Nuts

Ingredients:

For the Cake:

- 1 1/2 cups all-purpose flour
- 1 cup ground nuts (such as walnuts, almonds, or a mix)
- 1/2 cup granulated sugar
- 1/2 cup honey
- 1/2 cup unsalted butter, softened
- 2 large eggs
- 1/2 cup Greek yogurt or sour cream
- 1 tsp baking powder
- 1/2 tsp baking soda
- 1/2 tsp vanilla extract
- 1/2 tsp ground cinnamon (optional)
- 1/4 tsp salt

For the Honey Glaze:

- 1/2 cup honey
- 1/4 cup water
- 1/4 cup granulated sugar
- 1/2 tsp vanilla extract

Instructions:

1. **Preheat Oven:**
   - Preheat your oven to 350°F (175°C). Grease and flour a 9-inch round or square cake pan, or line it with parchment paper.
2. **Prepare the Cake Batter:**
   - In a medium bowl, whisk together the flour, baking powder, baking soda, salt, and ground cinnamon (if using). Set aside.
   - In a large bowl, beat the softened butter and granulated sugar until creamy and light.
   - Beat in the eggs one at a time, mixing well after each addition.
   - Mix in the honey, Greek yogurt (or sour cream), and vanilla extract until smooth.
   - Gradually add the dry ingredients to the wet ingredients, mixing until just combined.
   - Fold in the ground nuts.
3. **Bake the Cake:**
   - Pour the batter into the prepared cake pan and smooth the top.
   - Bake for 35-40 minutes, or until a toothpick inserted into the center comes out clean and the cake is golden brown.

- Allow the cake to cool in the pan for 10 minutes, then transfer to a wire rack to cool completely.
4. **Prepare the Honey Glaze:**
    - While the cake is cooling, combine honey, water, and granulated sugar in a small saucepan.
    - Bring to a boil over medium heat, stirring frequently, until the sugar is dissolved and the glaze thickens slightly, about 5-7 minutes. Stir in the vanilla extract. Let it cool.
5. **Glaze the Cake:**
    - Once the cake is completely cooled, brush the honey glaze evenly over the top and sides of the cake.
6. **Serve:**
    - Let the glaze set for a few minutes before slicing and serving.

Enjoy your Honey Cake with Nuts, a sweet and nutty treat that's sure to be a hit with anyone who loves rich, flavorful desserts!

Pistachio Cake

Ingredients:

For the Cake:

- 1 cup unsalted pistachios (shelled and roughly chopped)
- 1 1/2 cups all-purpose flour
- 1 cup granulated sugar
- 1/2 cup unsalted butter, softened
- 1/2 cup Greek yogurt or sour cream
- 3 large eggs
- 1 tsp baking powder
- 1/2 tsp baking soda
- 1/4 tsp salt
- 1/2 tsp vanilla extract
- 1/2 cup milk

For the Pistachio Glaze (Optional):

- 1/2 cup powdered sugar
- 2-3 tbsp milk
- 1/4 cup finely ground pistachios (for garnish)

Instructions:

1. **Preheat Oven:**
    - Preheat your oven to 350°F (175°C). Grease and flour a 9-inch round or square cake pan, or line it with parchment paper.
2. **Prepare the Pistachios:**
    - Roughly chop the pistachios. Set aside 1/4 cup for garnish if using.
3. **Prepare the Cake Batter:**
    - In a medium bowl, whisk together flour, baking powder, baking soda, and salt. Set aside.
    - In a large bowl, beat the softened butter and granulated sugar until light and fluffy.
    - Beat in the eggs one at a time, mixing well after each addition.
    - Mix in the Greek yogurt (or sour cream) and vanilla extract.
    - Gradually add the dry ingredients to the wet ingredients, alternating with the milk, until just combined.
    - Gently fold in the chopped pistachios.
4. **Bake the Cake:**
    - Pour the batter into the prepared cake pan and smooth the top.
    - Bake for 30-35 minutes, or until a toothpick inserted into the center comes out clean and the cake is golden brown.

- Allow the cake to cool in the pan for 10 minutes before transferring it to a wire rack to cool completely.
5. **Prepare the Glaze (Optional):**
    - In a small bowl, whisk together powdered sugar and milk until smooth and pourable. Add more milk if needed to reach the desired consistency.
6. **Glaze and Garnish:**
    - Once the cake has cooled, drizzle the pistachio glaze over the top.
    - Sprinkle the remaining chopped pistachios over the glaze for garnish.
7. **Serve:**
    - Slice and serve the cake at room temperature.

Enjoy your Pistachio Cake with its nutty flavor and delightful texture! It's perfect with a cup of tea or coffee.

Date Cake

Ingredients:

For the Cake:

- 1 cup pitted dates, chopped
- 1 cup boiling water
- 1/2 tsp baking soda
- 1/2 cup unsalted butter, softened
- 1/2 cup granulated sugar
- 1/2 cup brown sugar, packed
- 2 large eggs
- 1 tsp vanilla extract
- 1 1/2 cups all-purpose flour
- 1 1/2 tsp baking powder
- 1/4 tsp salt
- 1/2 tsp ground cinnamon (optional)
- 1/2 cup chopped nuts (optional, such as walnuts or pecans)

For the Topping (Optional):

- 1/4 cup brown sugar
- 1/4 cup chopped nuts

Instructions:

1. **Preheat Oven:**
   - Preheat your oven to 350°F (175°C). Grease and flour a 9-inch round or square baking pan, or line it with parchment paper.
2. **Prepare the Dates:**
   - Place the chopped dates in a bowl. Pour the boiling water over the dates and stir in the baking soda. Let it sit for about 10 minutes until the dates are softened and the mixture is slightly thickened.
3. **Prepare the Cake Batter:**
   - In a large bowl, cream together the softened butter, granulated sugar, and brown sugar until light and fluffy.
   - Beat in the eggs one at a time, mixing well after each addition. Stir in the vanilla extract.
   - In a separate bowl, whisk together the flour, baking powder, salt, and ground cinnamon (if using).
   - Gradually add the dry ingredients to the wet ingredients, mixing until just combined.
   - Fold in the date mixture and chopped nuts (if using).
4. **Bake the Cake:**

- Pour the batter into the prepared baking pan and smooth the top.
- Bake for 30-35 minutes, or until a toothpick inserted into the center comes out clean and the cake is golden brown.

5. **Prepare the Topping (Optional):**
    - While the cake is baking, mix the brown sugar with chopped nuts. Sprinkle this mixture over the cake about 5 minutes before the cake is done baking to allow it to caramelize.

6. **Cool and Serve:**
    - Allow the cake to cool in the pan for about 10 minutes before transferring it to a wire rack to cool completely.
    - Serve warm or at room temperature.

Enjoy your Date Cake with its rich, sweet flavor and moist texture!

Greek Walnut Cake

Ingredients:

For the Cake:

- 1 1/2 cups walnuts, finely chopped
- 1 cup all-purpose flour
- 1 tsp baking powder
- 1/2 tsp ground cinnamon
- 1/4 tsp ground cloves (optional)
- 1/4 tsp salt
- 1/2 cup unsalted butter, softened
- 1 cup granulated sugar
- 3 large eggs
- 1/2 cup Greek yogurt or sour cream
- 1/4 cup milk
- 1 tsp vanilla extract

For the Syrup:

- 1 cup granulated sugar
- 1 cup water
- 1/4 cup honey
- 1/2 tsp vanilla extract
- 1 cinnamon stick (optional)

Instructions:

1. **Preheat Oven:**
    - Preheat your oven to 350°F (175°C). Grease and flour a 9-inch round or square baking pan, or line it with parchment paper.
2. **Prepare the Cake Batter:**
    - In a medium bowl, whisk together the flour, baking powder, cinnamon, cloves (if using), and salt. Set aside.
    - In a large bowl, beat the softened butter and granulated sugar until light and fluffy.
    - Beat in the eggs one at a time, mixing well after each addition.
    - Mix in the Greek yogurt (or sour cream), milk, and vanilla extract until smooth.
    - Gradually add the dry ingredients to the wet ingredients, mixing until just combined.
    - Fold in the finely chopped walnuts.
3. **Bake the Cake:**
    - Pour the batter into the prepared baking pan and smooth the top.

- Bake for 35-40 minutes, or until a toothpick inserted into the center comes out clean and the cake is golden brown.
4. **Prepare the Syrup:**
    - While the cake is baking, combine sugar, water, honey, and cinnamon stick (if using) in a saucepan.
    - Bring to a boil, then reduce the heat and simmer for about 10 minutes, or until the syrup thickens slightly. Stir in the vanilla extract. Let it cool.
5. **Syrup the Cake:**
    - Once the cake is baked and still warm, pour the cooled syrup evenly over the cake.
    - Allow the cake to absorb the syrup and cool completely before serving.
6. **Serve:**
    - Cut into squares or slices and serve. The cake can be enjoyed at room temperature or slightly warm.

Enjoy your Greek Walnut Cake, a delightful blend of spiced nuts and sweet syrup!

Mastic Cake

Ingredients:

For the Cake:

- 1 1/2 cups all-purpose flour
- 1 1/2 tsp baking powder
- 1/2 tsp salt
- 1/2 cup unsalted butter, softened
- 1 cup granulated sugar
- 3 large eggs
- 1/2 cup Greek yogurt or sour cream
- 1/2 cup milk
- 1 tsp vanilla extract
- 1 tsp mastic resin, ground (you can use a mortar and pestle or a spice grinder)
- 1/4 tsp ground cinnamon (optional)

For the Glaze (Optional):

- 1/2 cup powdered sugar
- 1-2 tbsp milk or lemon juice
- 1/2 tsp vanilla extract

Instructions:

1. **Preheat Oven:**
   - Preheat your oven to 350°F (175°C). Grease and flour a 9-inch round or square baking pan, or line it with parchment paper.
2. **Prepare the Dry Ingredients:**
   - In a medium bowl, whisk together flour, baking powder, salt, and ground mastic resin. Set aside.
3. **Cream the Butter and Sugar:**
   - In a large bowl, beat the softened butter and granulated sugar until light and fluffy.
4. **Add Eggs and Wet Ingredients:**
   - Beat in the eggs one at a time, mixing well after each addition.
   - Mix in the Greek yogurt (or sour cream), milk, and vanilla extract until smooth.
5. **Combine Dry and Wet Ingredients:**
   - Gradually add the dry ingredients to the wet ingredients, mixing until just combined.
   - Fold in the ground mastic resin and ground cinnamon (if using).
6. **Bake the Cake:**
   - Pour the batter into the prepared cake pan and smooth the top.

- Bake for 30-35 minutes, or until a toothpick inserted into the center comes out clean and the cake is golden brown.

7. **Prepare the Glaze (Optional):**
    - In a small bowl, whisk together powdered sugar, milk or lemon juice, and vanilla extract until smooth and pourable.

8. **Cool and Glaze the Cake:**
    - Allow the cake to cool in the pan for about 10 minutes, then transfer it to a wire rack to cool completely.
    - If using, drizzle the glaze over the cooled cake.

9. **Serve:**
    - Slice and serve at room temperature. The cake can be stored in an airtight container for several days.

Enjoy your Mastic Cake, with its distinctive flavor and aromatic sweetness that's truly unique

Pistachio-Lemon Cake

Ingredients:

For the Cake:

- 1 cup shelled pistachios (finely ground)
- 1 1/2 cups all-purpose flour
- 1 tsp baking powder
- 1/2 tsp baking soda
- 1/4 tsp salt
- 1/2 cup unsalted butter, softened
- 1 cup granulated sugar
- 3 large eggs
- 1/2 cup Greek yogurt or sour cream
- 1/4 cup milk
- 1/4 cup lemon juice (freshly squeezed)
- 1 tbsp lemon zest (from about 1 lemon)
- 1/2 tsp vanilla extract

For the Lemon Glaze:

- 1 cup powdered sugar
- 2-3 tbsp lemon juice (or to taste)
- 1 tsp lemon zest (optional)

Instructions:

1. **Preheat Oven:**
   - Preheat your oven to 350°F (175°C). Grease and flour a 9-inch round or square baking pan, or line it with parchment paper.
2. **Prepare the Dry Ingredients:**
   - In a medium bowl, whisk together flour, baking powder, baking soda, and salt. Set aside.
3. **Cream the Butter and Sugar:**
   - In a large bowl, beat the softened butter and granulated sugar until light and fluffy.
4. **Add Eggs and Wet Ingredients:**
   - Beat in the eggs one at a time, mixing well after each addition.
   - Mix in the Greek yogurt (or sour cream), milk, lemon juice, lemon zest, and vanilla extract until smooth.
5. **Combine Dry and Wet Ingredients:**
   - Gradually add the dry ingredients to the wet ingredients, mixing until just combined.
   - Fold in the finely ground pistachios.

6. **Bake the Cake:**
   - Pour the batter into the prepared cake pan and smooth the top.
   - Bake for 30-35 minutes, or until a toothpick inserted into the center comes out clean and the cake is golden brown.
7. **Prepare the Lemon Glaze:**
   - In a small bowl, whisk together powdered sugar and lemon juice until smooth and pourable. Add more lemon juice if needed to reach the desired consistency. Stir in lemon zest if using.
8. **Cool and Glaze the Cake:**
   - Allow the cake to cool in the pan for about 10 minutes, then transfer it to a wire rack to cool completely.
   - Once the cake is cool, drizzle the lemon glaze over the top.
9. **Serve:**
   - Slice and serve at room temperature. The cake can be stored in an airtight container for several days.

Enjoy your Pistachio-Lemon Cake, a perfect blend of nutty and citrusy flavors!

Rosewater Cake

Ingredients:

For the Cake:

- 1 1/2 cups all-purpose flour
- 1 1/2 tsp baking powder
- 1/4 tsp salt
- 1/2 cup unsalted butter, softened
- 1 cup granulated sugar
- 2 large eggs
- 1/2 cup Greek yogurt or sour cream
- 1/4 cup milk
- 1-2 tbsp rosewater (adjust to taste)
- 1 tsp vanilla extract

For the Rosewater Glaze:

- 1 cup powdered sugar
- 2-3 tbsp milk or water
- 1-2 tbsp rosewater (adjust to taste)

For Garnish (Optional):

- Edible rose petals or dried rose petals
- Extra rosewater for a subtle drizzle

Instructions:

1. **Preheat Oven:**
   - Preheat your oven to 350°F (175°C). Grease and flour a 9-inch round or square baking pan, or line it with parchment paper.
2. **Prepare the Dry Ingredients:**
   - In a medium bowl, whisk together flour, baking powder, and salt. Set aside.
3. **Cream the Butter and Sugar:**
   - In a large bowl, beat the softened butter and granulated sugar until light and fluffy.
4. **Add Eggs and Wet Ingredients:**
   - Beat in the eggs one at a time, mixing well after each addition.
   - Mix in the Greek yogurt (or sour cream), milk, rosewater, and vanilla extract until smooth.
5. **Combine Dry and Wet Ingredients:**
   - Gradually add the dry ingredients to the wet ingredients, mixing until just combined.
6. **Bake the Cake:**

- Pour the batter into the prepared baking pan and smooth the top.
- Bake for 30-35 minutes, or until a toothpick inserted into the center comes out clean and the cake is golden brown.

7. **Prepare the Rosewater Glaze:**
   - In a small bowl, whisk together powdered sugar, milk or water, and rosewater until smooth and pourable. Adjust the amount of rosewater to taste.
8. **Cool and Glaze the Cake:**
   - Allow the cake to cool in the pan for about 10 minutes before transferring it to a wire rack to cool completely.
   - Once the cake is cool, drizzle the rosewater glaze over the top.
9. **Garnish and Serve:**
   - Garnish with edible rose petals or dried rose petals if desired.
   - Serve at room temperature.

Enjoy your Rosewater Cake, a delicate and aromatic dessert that's sure to impress!

Fig Cake

Ingredients:

For the Cake:

- 1 1/2 cups fresh figs (chopped) or 1 cup dried figs (chopped and soaked in warm water)
- 1 cup all-purpose flour
- 1/2 tsp baking powder
- 1/2 tsp baking soda
- 1/4 tsp salt
- 1/2 tsp ground cinnamon
- 1/4 tsp ground nutmeg (optional)
- 1/2 cup unsalted butter, softened
- 1 cup granulated sugar
- 2 large eggs
- 1/2 cup Greek yogurt or sour cream
- 1/4 cup milk
- 1 tsp vanilla extract
- 1/2 cup chopped nuts (optional, such as walnuts or pecans)

For the Glaze (Optional):

- 1/2 cup powdered sugar
- 2-3 tbsp milk or lemon juice
- 1/2 tsp vanilla extract

Instructions:

1. **Preheat Oven:**
   - Preheat your oven to 350°F (175°C). Grease and flour a 9-inch round or square cake pan, or line it with parchment paper.
2. **Prepare the Figs:**
   - If using fresh figs, chop them into small pieces. If using dried figs, chop them and soak in warm water for about 10 minutes, then drain.
3. **Prepare the Dry Ingredients:**
   - In a medium bowl, whisk together flour, baking powder, baking soda, salt, cinnamon, and nutmeg (if using). Set aside.
4. **Cream the Butter and Sugar:**
   - In a large bowl, beat the softened butter and granulated sugar until light and fluffy.
5. **Add Eggs and Wet Ingredients:**
   - Beat in the eggs one at a time, mixing well after each addition.
   - Mix in the Greek yogurt (or sour cream), milk, and vanilla extract until smooth.
6. **Combine Dry and Wet Ingredients:**

- Gradually add the dry ingredients to the wet ingredients, mixing until just combined.
- Fold in the chopped figs and nuts (if using).

7. **Bake the Cake:**
   - Pour the batter into the prepared cake pan and smooth the top.
   - Bake for 35-40 minutes, or until a toothpick inserted into the center comes out clean and the cake is golden brown.
8. **Prepare the Glaze (Optional):**
   - In a small bowl, whisk together powdered sugar and milk or lemon juice until smooth and pourable. Stir in vanilla extract.
9. **Cool and Glaze the Cake:**
   - Allow the cake to cool in the pan for about 10 minutes before transferring it to a wire rack to cool completely.
   - Once the cake is cool, drizzle the glaze over the top if desired.
10. **Serve:**
    - Slice and serve the cake at room temperature.

Enjoy your Fig Cake, a delightful dessert that combines the natural sweetness of figs with a moist, tender crumb!

Greek Cream Cake

Ingredients:

For the Cake Base:

- 1 cup all-purpose flour
- 1/2 cup granulated sugar
- 1/2 cup unsalted butter, softened
- 2 large eggs
- 1 tsp baking powder
- 1/4 tsp salt
- 1/4 cup milk
- 1 tsp vanilla extract

For the Cream Filling:

- 2 cups milk
- 1/2 cup granulated sugar
- 1/4 cup cornstarch
- 3 large egg yolks
- 2 tbsp unsalted butter
- 1 tsp vanilla extract

For the Topping:

- Fresh fruit (such as berries or sliced peaches)
- Powdered sugar (for dusting)
- Optional: chopped nuts or a drizzle of honey

Instructions:

1. **Preheat Oven:**
    - Preheat your oven to 350°F (175°C). Grease and flour a 9-inch round or square baking pan.
2. **Prepare the Cake Base:**
    - In a medium bowl, whisk together flour, baking powder, and salt. Set aside.
    - In a large bowl, cream the softened butter and granulated sugar until light and fluffy.
    - Beat in the eggs one at a time, mixing well after each addition.
    - Mix in the milk and vanilla extract until smooth.
    - Gradually add the dry ingredients to the wet ingredients, mixing until just combined.
    - Pour the batter into the prepared baking pan and smooth the top.
    - Bake for 20-25 minutes, or until a toothpick inserted into the center comes out clean and the cake is golden brown.

- Allow the cake to cool completely in the pan on a wire rack.
3. **Prepare the Cream Filling:**
    - In a medium saucepan, heat the milk until just steaming (do not boil).
    - In a separate bowl, whisk together sugar, cornstarch, and egg yolks.
    - Slowly add the hot milk to the egg mixture, whisking constantly.
    - Return the mixture to the saucepan and cook over medium heat, stirring constantly, until it thickens and starts to bubble.
    - Remove from heat and stir in the butter and vanilla extract until smooth.
    - Let the cream filling cool to room temperature.
4. **Assemble the Cake:**
    - Once the cake is cool, spread the cream filling evenly over the top.
    - Decorate with fresh fruit and sprinkle with powdered sugar. Add chopped nuts or a drizzle of honey if desired.
5. **Serve:**
    - Chill the cake in the refrigerator for at least an hour before serving to allow the cream to set.

Enjoy your Greek Cream Cake, a deliciously creamy and elegant dessert that's perfect for any occasion!

Almond and Orange Cake

Ingredients:

For the Cake:

- 1 cup ground almonds (almond meal)
- 1 cup all-purpose flour
- 1 1/2 tsp baking powder
- 1/4 tsp salt
- 1/2 cup unsalted butter, softened
- 1 cup granulated sugar
- 3 large eggs
- 1/2 cup Greek yogurt or sour cream
- 1/4 cup orange juice (freshly squeezed)
- 1 tbsp orange zest (from about 1 orange)
- 1 tsp vanilla extract

For the Orange Syrup (Optional):

- 1/2 cup granulated sugar
- 1/2 cup orange juice
- 1 tsp orange zest

Instructions:

1. **Preheat Oven:**
    - Preheat your oven to 350°F (175°C). Grease and flour a 9-inch round or square cake pan, or line it with parchment paper.
2. **Prepare the Dry Ingredients:**
    - In a medium bowl, whisk together the flour, baking powder, and salt. Set aside.
3. **Cream the Butter and Sugar:**
    - In a large bowl, beat the softened butter and granulated sugar until light and fluffy.
4. **Add Eggs and Wet Ingredients:**
    - Beat in the eggs one at a time, mixing well after each addition.
    - Mix in the Greek yogurt (or sour cream), orange juice, orange zest, and vanilla extract until smooth.
5. **Combine Dry and Wet Ingredients:**
    - Gradually add the dry ingredients to the wet ingredients, mixing until just combined.
    - Fold in the ground almonds.
6. **Bake the Cake:**
    - Pour the batter into the prepared cake pan and smooth the top.

- Bake for 30-35 minutes, or until a toothpick inserted into the center comes out clean and the cake is golden brown.
7. **Prepare the Orange Syrup (Optional):**
    - While the cake is baking, combine sugar, orange juice, and orange zest in a small saucepan.
    - Bring to a boil, then reduce the heat and simmer for about 5-7 minutes, until the syrup thickens slightly. Let it cool.
8. **Cool and Glaze the Cake:**
    - Allow the cake to cool in the pan for about 10 minutes before transferring it to a wire rack to cool completely.
    - If using, brush the cooled cake with the orange syrup to add extra flavor and moisture.
9. **Serve:**
    - Slice and serve the cake at room temperature. It's perfect on its own or with a dusting of powdered sugar.

Enjoy your Almond and Orange Cake, a delightful combination of nutty and citrus flavors!

Lemon Honey Cake

Ingredients:

For the Cake:

- 1 1/2 cups all-purpose flour
- 1 tsp baking powder
- 1/2 tsp baking soda
- 1/4 tsp salt
- 1/2 cup unsalted butter, softened
- 1/2 cup honey
- 1/2 cup granulated sugar
- 2 large eggs
- 1/2 cup Greek yogurt or sour cream
- 1/4 cup lemon juice (freshly squeezed)
- 1 tbsp lemon zest (from about 1 lemon)
- 1 tsp vanilla extract

For the Lemon Honey Glaze:

- 1/2 cup honey
- 2 tbsp lemon juice
- 1/2 tsp lemon zest (optional)

Instructions:

1. **Preheat Oven:**
   - Preheat your oven to 350°F (175°C). Grease and flour a 9-inch round or square baking pan, or line it with parchment paper.
2. **Prepare the Dry Ingredients:**
   - In a medium bowl, whisk together flour, baking powder, baking soda, and salt. Set aside.
3. **Cream the Butter and Sugars:**
   - In a large bowl, beat the softened butter, honey, and granulated sugar until light and fluffy.
4. **Add Eggs and Wet Ingredients:**
   - Beat in the eggs one at a time, mixing well after each addition.
   - Mix in the Greek yogurt (or sour cream), lemon juice, lemon zest, and vanilla extract until smooth.
5. **Combine Dry and Wet Ingredients:**
   - Gradually add the dry ingredients to the wet ingredients, mixing until just combined.
6. **Bake the Cake:**
   - Pour the batter into the prepared pan and smooth the top.

- Bake for 30-35 minutes, or until a toothpick inserted into the center comes out clean and the cake is golden brown.
7. **Prepare the Lemon Honey Glaze:**
    - In a small saucepan, heat honey and lemon juice over low heat until combined and smooth. Add lemon zest if desired.
8. **Cool and Glaze the Cake:**
    - Allow the cake to cool in the pan for about 10 minutes before transferring it to a wire rack to cool completely.
    - Brush or drizzle the warm lemon honey glaze over the cooled cake.
9. **Serve:**
    - Slice and serve the cake at room temperature.

Enjoy your Lemon Honey Cake, with its delightful balance of tangy and sweet flavors!

Greek Yogurt and Honey Cake

Ingredients:

For the Cake:

- 1 1/2 cups all-purpose flour
- 1 1/2 tsp baking powder
- 1/2 tsp baking soda
- 1/4 tsp salt
- 1/2 cup unsalted butter, softened
- 1/2 cup granulated sugar
- 1/2 cup honey
- 2 large eggs
- 1 cup Greek yogurt (plain or vanilla)
- 1/4 cup milk
- 1 tsp vanilla extract

For the Honey Glaze (Optional):

- 1/2 cup honey
- 2 tbsp water or lemon juice
- 1/2 tsp vanilla extract (optional)

Instructions:

1. **Preheat Oven:**
   - Preheat your oven to 350°F (175°C). Grease and flour a 9-inch round or square baking pan, or line it with parchment paper.
2. **Prepare the Dry Ingredients:**
   - In a medium bowl, whisk together flour, baking powder, baking soda, and salt. Set aside.
3. **Cream the Butter and Sugars:**
   - In a large bowl, beat the softened butter, granulated sugar, and honey until light and fluffy.
4. **Add Eggs and Wet Ingredients:**
   - Beat in the eggs one at a time, mixing well after each addition.
   - Mix in the Greek yogurt, milk, and vanilla extract until smooth.
5. **Combine Dry and Wet Ingredients:**
   - Gradually add the dry ingredients to the wet ingredients, mixing until just combined.
6. **Bake the Cake:**
   - Pour the batter into the prepared pan and smooth the top.
   - Bake for 30-35 minutes, or until a toothpick inserted into the center comes out clean and the cake is golden brown.

7. **Prepare the Honey Glaze (Optional):**
    - In a small saucepan, gently heat honey with water or lemon juice until smooth and slightly thin. Stir in vanilla extract if desired.
8. **Cool and Glaze the Cake:**
    - Allow the cake to cool in the pan for about 10 minutes before transferring it to a wire rack to cool completely.
    - Brush or drizzle the honey glaze over the cooled cake.
9. **Serve:**
    - Slice and serve the cake at room temperature. It's great on its own or with a dollop of Greek yogurt or fresh fruit.

Enjoy your Greek Yogurt and Honey Cake, a moist and sweet treat that combines the best of yogurt and honey flavors!

Greek Chocolate and Nut Cake

Ingredients:

For the Cake:

- 1 cup all-purpose flour
- 1/2 cup unsweetened cocoa powder
- 1 tsp baking powder
- 1/2 tsp baking soda
- 1/4 tsp salt
- 1/2 cup unsalted butter, softened
- 1 cup granulated sugar
- 2 large eggs
- 1/2 cup Greek yogurt or sour cream
- 1/2 cup milk
- 1 tsp vanilla extract
- 1 cup chopped nuts (such as walnuts, almonds, or hazelnuts)
- 1/2 cup semi-sweet chocolate chips (optional)

For the Ganache (Optional):

- 1/2 cup heavy cream
- 4 oz semi-sweet chocolate, chopped
- 1 tbsp unsalted butter (optional, for added shine)

Instructions:

1. **Preheat Oven:**
   - Preheat your oven to 350°F (175°C). Grease and flour a 9-inch round or square baking pan, or line it with parchment paper.
2. **Prepare the Dry Ingredients:**
   - In a medium bowl, whisk together flour, cocoa powder, baking powder, baking soda, and salt. Set aside.
3. **Cream the Butter and Sugar:**
   - In a large bowl, beat the softened butter and granulated sugar until light and fluffy.
4. **Add Eggs and Wet Ingredients:**
   - Beat in the eggs one at a time, mixing well after each addition.
   - Mix in the Greek yogurt (or sour cream), milk, and vanilla extract until smooth.
5. **Combine Dry and Wet Ingredients:**
   - Gradually add the dry ingredients to the wet ingredients, mixing until just combined.
   - Fold in the chopped nuts and chocolate chips (if using).
6. **Bake the Cake:**

- Pour the batter into the prepared pan and smooth the top.
- Bake for 30-35 minutes, or until a toothpick inserted into the center comes out clean and the cake is set.

7. **Prepare the Ganache (Optional):**
   - In a small saucepan, heat the heavy cream until just steaming. Remove from heat and add the chopped chocolate. Let sit for a few minutes, then stir until smooth.
   - Stir in the butter if using, for extra shine.

8. **Cool and Frost the Cake:**
   - Allow the cake to cool in the pan for about 10 minutes before transferring it to a wire rack to cool completely.
   - Once cool, pour the ganache over the cake and spread it evenly.

9. **Serve:**
   - Slice and serve the cake at room temperature. It pairs well with a dollop of whipped cream or a scoop of vanilla ice cream.

Enjoy your Greek Chocolate and Nut Cake, a rich and delightful treat with a wonderful blend of chocolate and nuts!

Baklava Bundt Cake

Ingredients:

For the Cake:

- 1 1/2 cups all-purpose flour
- 1/2 tsp baking powder
- 1/2 tsp baking soda
- 1/4 tsp salt
- 1/2 cup unsalted butter, softened
- 1 cup granulated sugar
- 3 large eggs
- 1/2 cup Greek yogurt or sour cream
- 1/4 cup milk
- 1 tsp vanilla extract
- 1 tsp ground cinnamon

For the Nut Filling:

- 1 cup finely chopped nuts (such as walnuts, almonds, or pistachios)
- 1/4 cup granulated sugar
- 1/2 tsp ground cinnamon
- 1/4 tsp ground cloves (optional)

For the Honey Glaze:

- 1/2 cup honey
- 2 tbsp water
- 1/4 tsp ground cinnamon
- 1/4 cup chopped nuts for garnish (optional)

Instructions:

1. **Preheat Oven:**
    - Preheat your oven to 350°F (175°C). Grease and flour a Bundt pan, making sure to get into all the crevices to prevent sticking.
2. **Prepare the Nut Filling:**
    - In a small bowl, mix together the chopped nuts, granulated sugar, ground cinnamon, and ground cloves (if using). Set aside.
3. **Prepare the Cake Batter:**
    - In a medium bowl, whisk together the flour, baking powder, baking soda, salt, and ground cinnamon. Set aside.
    - In a large bowl, cream the softened butter and granulated sugar until light and fluffy.
    - Beat in the eggs one at a time, mixing well after each addition.

- Mix in the Greek yogurt (or sour cream), milk, and vanilla extract until smooth.
- Gradually add the dry ingredients to the wet ingredients, mixing until just combined.

4. **Assemble the Cake:**
   - Spoon about a third of the cake batter into the prepared Bundt pan and spread it evenly.
   - Sprinkle half of the nut filling over the batter.
   - Add another third of the cake batter and spread it evenly.
   - Sprinkle the remaining nut filling over the batter.
   - Top with the remaining cake batter and smooth the top.
5. **Bake the Cake:**
   - Bake for 40-50 minutes, or until a toothpick inserted into the center comes out clean and the cake is golden brown.
6. **Prepare the Honey Glaze:**
   - While the cake is baking, in a small saucepan, heat honey and water over low heat until combined and warmed. Stir in ground cinnamon.
7. **Cool and Glaze the Cake:**
   - Allow the cake to cool in the pan for about 10 minutes before transferring it to a wire rack to cool completely.
   - Once the cake is cool, brush or drizzle the warm honey glaze over the cake.
   - Garnish with additional chopped nuts if desired.
8. **Serve:**
   - Slice and serve the cake at room temperature.

Enjoy your Baklava Bundt Cake, a delightful fusion of the classic flavors of baklava with the easy elegance of a Bundt cake!

Olive Oil Cake

Ingredients:

- 1 1/2 cups all-purpose flour
- 1 cup granulated sugar
- 1 1/2 tsp baking powder
- 1/2 tsp baking soda
- 1/4 tsp salt
- 1/2 cup extra-virgin olive oil
- 3 large eggs
- 1/2 cup milk (whole or 2%)
- 1/2 cup Greek yogurt or sour cream
- 1 tsp vanilla extract
- 1/4 cup freshly squeezed lemon juice (or orange juice for a different twist)
- 1 tbsp lemon zest (or orange zest)
- Optional: 1/4 cup sliced almonds or chopped nuts for topping

For the Glaze (Optional):

- 1/2 cup powdered sugar
- 2-3 tbsp lemon juice (or orange juice)
- 1 tsp vanilla extract

Instructions:

1. **Preheat Oven:**
   - Preheat your oven to 350°F (175°C). Grease and flour a 9-inch round or square baking pan, or line it with parchment paper.
2. **Prepare Dry Ingredients:**
   - In a medium bowl, whisk together flour, granulated sugar, baking powder, baking soda, and salt. Set aside.
3. **Mix Wet Ingredients:**
   - In a large bowl, whisk together the olive oil, eggs, milk, Greek yogurt (or sour cream), vanilla extract, lemon juice, and lemon zest until well combined.
4. **Combine Dry and Wet Ingredients:**
   - Gradually add the dry ingredients to the wet ingredients, mixing until just combined. Be careful not to overmix.
5. **Bake the Cake:**
   - Pour the batter into the prepared pan and smooth the top.
   - If desired, sprinkle sliced almonds or chopped nuts on top of the batter for added texture and flavor.
   - Bake for 30-35 minutes, or until a toothpick inserted into the center comes out clean and the cake is golden brown.
6. **Cool the Cake:**

- Allow the cake to cool in the pan for about 10 minutes before transferring it to a wire rack to cool completely.
7. **Prepare the Glaze (Optional):**
   - In a small bowl, whisk together powdered sugar, lemon juice (or orange juice), and vanilla extract until smooth. Adjust the consistency by adding more juice or powdered sugar as needed.
8. **Glaze the Cake:**
   - Once the cake is completely cooled, drizzle the glaze over the top.
9. **Serve:**
   - Slice and serve the cake at room temperature.

Enjoy your Olive Oil Cake, a wonderfully moist and flavorful treat that's perfect for any time of year!

Pomegranate Cake

Ingredients:

For the Cake:

- 1 1/2 cups all-purpose flour
- 1 tsp baking powder
- 1/2 tsp baking soda
- 1/4 tsp salt
- 1/2 cup unsalted butter, softened
- 1 cup granulated sugar
- 2 large eggs
- 1/2 cup Greek yogurt or sour cream
- 1/2 cup pomegranate juice (preferably fresh)
- 1/4 cup pomegranate seeds
- 1 tsp vanilla extract

For the Pomegranate Glaze (Optional):

- 1/2 cup powdered sugar
- 2-3 tbsp pomegranate juice
- 1/4 tsp vanilla extract

Instructions:

1. **Preheat Oven:**
   - Preheat your oven to 350°F (175°C). Grease and flour a 9-inch round or square baking pan, or line it with parchment paper.
2. **Prepare Dry Ingredients:**
   - In a medium bowl, whisk together flour, baking powder, baking soda, and salt. Set aside.
3. **Cream the Butter and Sugar:**
   - In a large bowl, beat the softened butter and granulated sugar until light and fluffy.
4. **Add Eggs and Wet Ingredients:**
   - Beat in the eggs one at a time, mixing well after each addition.
   - Mix in the Greek yogurt (or sour cream), pomegranate juice, and vanilla extract until smooth.
5. **Combine Dry and Wet Ingredients:**
   - Gradually add the dry ingredients to the wet ingredients, mixing until just combined.
   - Gently fold in the pomegranate seeds.
6. **Bake the Cake:**
   - Pour the batter into the prepared pan and smooth the top.

- Bake for 30-35 minutes, or until a toothpick inserted into the center comes out clean and the cake is golden brown.
7. **Cool the Cake:**
    - Allow the cake to cool in the pan for about 10 minutes before transferring it to a wire rack to cool completely.
8. **Prepare the Pomegranate Glaze (Optional):**
    - In a small bowl, whisk together powdered sugar, pomegranate juice, and vanilla extract until smooth.
9. **Glaze the Cake:**
    - Once the cake is completely cooled, drizzle the glaze over the top.
10. **Serve:**
    - Slice and serve the cake at room temperature, optionally garnished with additional pomegranate seeds for a festive touch.

Enjoy your Pomegranate Cake, a deliciously tangy and sweet treat perfect for any occasion!